Responsive Media in HTML5

Learn effective administration of responsive media within your website or CMS system using practical techniques

Alex Libby

PUBLISHING

BIRMINGHAM - MUMBAI

Responsive Media in HTML5

First published: December 2014

Production reference: 1201214

Published by Packt Publishing Ltd.
Livery Place
35 Livery Street
Birmingham B3 2PB, UK.

ISBN 978-1-84969-696-8

www.packtpub.com

Credits

Author
Alex Libby

Reviewers
Tristan Denyer
Vaibhav Kanwal
Marija Zaric

Acquisition Editors
Harsha Bharwani
James Jones

Content Development Editor
Rohit Kumar Singh

Technical Editors
Pragnesh Bilimoria
Shruti Rawool

Copy Editor
Laxmi Subramanian

Project Coordinator
Mary Alex

Proofreaders
Simran Bhogal
Maria Gould
Ameesha Green

Indexer
Monica Ajmera Mehta

Production Coordinator
Nilesh R. Mohite

Cover Work
Nilesh R. Mohite

About the Author

Alex Libby has a background in IT support. He has been involved in supporting end users for the last 18 years in a variety of different environments and currently works as a technical analyst, supporting a medium-sized SharePoint estate for an international parts distributor based in the UK. Although he gets to play with different technologies in his day job, his first true love has always been the open source movement, in particular, experimenting with CSS/CSS3 and HTML5. So far, he has written several books for Packt Publishing, including one on HTML5 video and another on the jQuery UI. This is his eighth book.

I'd like to thank family and friends for their help and encouragement and the reviewers for providing lots of constructive comments — without them, I am sure I wouldn't have been able to produce this book!

About the Reviewers

Tristan Denyer is a UX designer for web and mobile, including web apps and portals, e-commerce, online video players and widgets, games (online, iPhone, and board), marketing sites, and more. He's also a UI developer and a WordPress theme developer. He is currently leading the UX/UI for the product team at a start-up in San Francisco. He recently wrote *A Practical Handbook for WordPress Themes, CreateSpace Independent Publishing Platform* to help owners and operators of self-hosted WordPress websites get the most out of their themes.

His passions include prototyping, web security, writing, carpentry, burritos, and maintaining his popular jQuery plugin on GitHub that helps duplicate a section of a form. He can be found on Twitter at @tristandenyer and on GitHub at https://github.com/tristandenyer, and he blogs at http://tristandenyer.com/.

Marija Zaric is a web designer living in Belgrade with a focus on individual and commercial clients who demand websites that are clear, modern, creative, simple, and responsive. She works with clients from the USA and all over the world, helping them present their services in a unique yet professional way.

Years ago, she started experimenting with Dreamweaver, CSS, and XHTML. She became very fond of coding and retro design. This influenced her to create her first website and achieve subsequent successes. Today, she is a relentless learner. What she loves the most about web design is the constant changes in the field, especially its evolution in the last 3 years when she got inspired by its simplicity, great images, typography, and the possibility to optimize a single website for various devices.

She redesigned and incorporated these styles into her own website and called it Creative Simplicity. With the development of HTML5, she made free templates that are used all over the world in order to advertise her work and share the knowledge. She predicts that in 2015, flat and modern web design will be here to stay, supported by nice photography, responsive design, and strong typography. Her projects can be found at http://www.marijazaric.com/ and http://creativesimplicitywebstudio.com/.

www.PacktPub.com

Support files, eBooks, discount offers, and more

For support files and downloads related to your book, please visit www.PacktPub.com.

Did you know that Packt offers eBook versions of every book published, with PDF and ePub files available? You can upgrade to the eBook version at www.PacktPub.com and as a print book customer, you are entitled to a discount on the eBook copy. Get in touch with us at service@packtpub.com for more details.

At www.PacktPub.com, you can also read a collection of free technical articles, sign up for a range of free newsletters and receive exclusive discounts and offers on Packt books and eBooks.

https://www2.packtpub.com/books/subscription/packtlib

Do you need instant solutions to your IT questions? PacktLib is Packt's online digital book library. Here, you can search, access, and read Packt's entire library of books.

Why subscribe?
- Fully searchable across every book published by Packt
- Copy and paste, print, and bookmark content
- On demand and accessible via a web browser

Free access for Packt account holders

If you have an account with Packt at www.PacktPub.com, you can use this to access PacktLib today and view 9 entirely free books. Simply use your login credentials for immediate access.

Table of Contents

Preface

Web design is responsive design. Responsive web design is web design done right.

– Andy Clarke, Stuff and Nonsense

Take a straw poll of one hundred users and it is likely you will find that a good proportion have viewed the Internet from a mobile device at some point in the past. Use of these devices to access the Internet has exploded massively over the last few years. This has highlighted the need to design sites that work well on a variety of different devices and platforms.

First coined as a term by Ethan Marcotte back in 2010, responsive web design is the art of designing such sites. A key element of responsive web design is the addition of images and videos. Throughout this book, we're going to take a look at the tips and tricks you need to get ahead in adding responsive media to your sites. We'll see how the lack of a common W3C standard means the field is wide open for different solutions and that catering for different platforms means understanding their limits and making suitable allowances for each type of device.

We'll work through a number of practical examples, with both images and videos, and see the importance of testing both to ensure your content displays as expected on any device. We'll then make use of some of the tips and tricks in several real-world examples, using popular frameworks such as WordPress or Less CSS—you'll see that adding responsive media isn't actually that complicated!

Question is though—are you ready to make a start?

What this book covers

Chapter 1, Working with Responsive Images, starts our journey with responsive media, where we take a look at working with responsive media. We'll cover the basics with a look at a wide variety of topics, including retina images, providing fallback support, different image formats to use, and catering to the differences between mobile and desktop platforms.

Chapter 2, Adding Responsive Video Content, continues on from where we left off in *Chapter 1, Working with Responsive Images*, with a look at adding responsive video to our sites. We'll cover the different formats available to us and the methods to be used to determine which one to use, how to determine the size of the video to use depending on viewport space, providing fallback support, and making allowances for different platforms.

Chapter 3, Mixing Content, helps us bring it all together with a look at some of the considerations or pitfalls of mixing responsive content and how we can reduce delays by using preloaders to control when content is loaded and rendered on screen. We'll work through an example of mixing both responsive images and video on the same page, so we can see how it works in practice and consider what allowances may need to be made for different platforms.

Chapter 4, Testing Responsive Media, delves into the world of testing our creations to ensure they work properly. We'll see that there is no need for complicated tools as most of our work can be done in a browser; we will also cover some tips to troubleshoot slow performance issues and how we can make quick and easy changes to help improve speed.

Chapter 5, Using Frameworks, finishes up the book with a look at three real-world examples of using responsive media in popular frameworks; our examples include a look at WordPress, Less CSS, and Bootstrap. We'll take a look at some of the tips and tricks (and plugins) available for use in WordPress, adding responsive media to a Bootstrap-enabled webpage, and how we can use Less CSS to help better manage our CSS styles.

What you need for this book

All you need to work through most of the examples in this book is a simple text or code editor and a browser (preferably Firefox with Firebug installed). I recommend installing Sublime Text—either Version 2 or 3—although if you have your own particular preference, that will be fine.

Some of the examples make use of additional software, such as WordPress or Crunch—the details of each are included within the appropriate chapter along with links to download the application from source.

Who this book is for

The book is for frontend developers who want to get up to speed on making media content responsive as part of building responsive websites. To get the most out of this book, you should have a good working knowledge of HTML, CSS, JavaScript, and ideally be comfortable using jQuery.

Some of the examples towards the end of the book use popular tools such as WordPress, Less CSS, and Bootstrap. Although it is assumed you will have some prior knowledge of each, the tips and tricks are not complex and could be picked up relatively easily.

Conventions

In this book, you will find a number of styles of text that distinguish between different kinds of information. Here are some examples of these styles and an explanation of their meaning.

Code words in text, database table names, folder names, filenames, file extensions, pathnames, dummy URLs, user input, and Twitter handles are shown as follows: "Catering for HD/Retina images and using the `<picture>` tags."

A block of code is set as follows:

```
img { max-width: 100%; height: auto; float: left; padding: 10px; }
#description { box-sizing: border-box; }
#peytoe { ... padding: 0px 10px 10px; width: 66%; }
```

When we wish to draw your attention to a particular part of a code block, the relevant lines or items are set in bold:

```
<title>Demo - Setting a viewport using CSS</title>
<meta name="viewport" content="width=360">
<link href="css/viewport-css.css" rel="stylesheet">
```

Any command-line input or output is written as follows:

```
npm install grunt-cli grunt-contrib-watch grunt-autoprefixer
```

New terms and important words are shown in bold. Words that you see on the screen, in menus or dialog boxes for example, appear in the text likes this: "Click on the cog, then select **Share and embed map**."

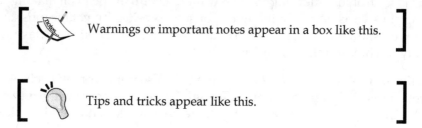

> Warnings or important notes appear in a box like this.

> Tips and tricks appear like this.

Reader feedback

Feedback from our readers is always welcome. Let us know what you think about this book—what you liked or disliked. Reader feedback is important for us as it helps us develop titles that you will really get the most out of.

To send us general feedback, simply e-mail feedback@packtpub.com, and mention the book's title in the subject of your message.

If there is a topic that you have expertise in and you are interested in either writing or contributing to a book, see our author guide at www.packtpub.com/authors.

Customer support

Now that you are the proud owner of a Packt book, we have a number of things to help you to get the most from your purchase.

Downloading the example code

You can download the example code files from your account at http://www.packtpub.com for all the Packt Publishing books you have purchased. If you purchased this book elsewhere, you can visit http://www.packtpub.com/support and register to have the files e-mailed directly to you.

Downloading the color images of this book

We also provide you with a PDF file that has color images of the screenshots/diagrams used in this book. The color images will help you better understand the changes in the output. You can download this file from: `http://www.packtpub.com/sites/default/files/downloads/6968OT_ColorImages.pdf`.

Errata

Although we have taken every care to ensure the accuracy of our content, mistakes do happen. If you find a mistake in one of our books—maybe a mistake in the text or the code—we would be grateful if you could report this to us. By doing so, you can save other readers from frustration and help us improve subsequent versions of this book. If you find any errata, please report them by visiting `http://www.packtpub.com/submit-errata`, selecting your book, clicking on the **Errata Submission Form** link, and entering the details of your errata. Once your errata are verified, your submission will be accepted and the errata will be uploaded to our website or added to any list of existing errata under the Errata section of that title.

To view the previously submitted errata, go to `https://www.packtpub.com/books/content/support` and enter the name of the book in the search field. The required information will appear under the **Errata** section.

Piracy

Piracy of copyrighted material on the Internet is an ongoing problem across all media. At Packt, we take the protection of our copyright and licenses very seriously. If you come across any illegal copies of our works in any form on the Internet, please provide us with the location address or website name immediately so that we can pursue a remedy.

Please contact us at `copyright@packtpub.com` with a link to the suspected pirated material.

We appreciate your help in protecting our authors and our ability to bring you valuable content.

Questions

If you have a problem with any aspect of this book, you can contact us at `questions@packtpub.com`, and we will do our best to address the problem.

1
Working with Responsive Images

"A picture tells a thousand words…"

These words used in an advert dating from 1913 for the Piqua Auto Supply House of Piqua, Ohio, still ring true over a hundred years later. The only difference is the advent of technology — with the increasing use of mobile phones, tablets, and portable devices comes a need to display content on smaller devices. While text might be easy to display, images are less so, but are still just as important. Throughout this chapter, we're going to look at some of the tips and tricks you need to learn in order to display images of the right size and quality on a variety of different devices.

Creating responsive images can be as easy or complex as needed. In this chapter, we will cover a host of topics, which include:

- Working with fluid images, icons, and sprites
- Catering to vendor prefixes, image formats, and different platforms
- Catering to HD/Retina images and using the `<picture>` tags
- Determining an available viewport for use
- Working out media queries using CSS, JavaScript, or data tags
- Building a responsive carousel and creating responsive maps

Curious? Let's get started!

Getting started

Throughout this chapter, we'll work using a project area. Before we get started, it is strongly recommended that you create a project folder. For the purposes of this chapter, I will assume it is called `code`; inside it, you will need to create four folders: `css`, `js`, `font`, and `img`, as shown in this screenshot:

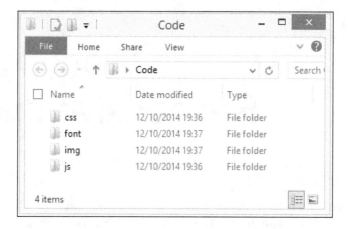

We will refer to the folders created here throughout the chapter.

Beginning with fluid images

How many times have you created web pages only to find that a viewer complains that they look poor on a mobile device? I'll bet that one possible reason for this is image content. The image is set with fixed sizes, so it doesn't resize well in smaller browsers, right?

In this tutorial, we will take a look at the basics needed to move away from fixed images to those that adapt when a browser window has been resized or content is being viewed on a mobile device.

For this exercise, I've created a dummy page about Lake Peyto in Canada—a truly stunning part of Canada if you are fortunate to be able to visit! Throughout this tutorial, we're going to make some changes to help make the image react better when resized in a browser window. These steps will guide you through the exercise:

1. Let's start by cracking open a copy of the code download and extracting `simplefluid1.html` and `simplefluid1.css`. This a simple web page about Lake Peyto, Canada.

2. Try resizing the browser window. Notice how it doesn't resize any of the content? Let's fix that by making two small changes to our code.

3. Alter the two lines in `simplefluid1.css` as shown in these lines of code:

```
img { max-width: 100%; height: auto; float: left; padding: 10px; }
#description { box-sizing: border-box; }
#peytoe { ... padding: 0px 10px 10px; width: 66%; }
```

The three changes we just performed are all that is required to make the content responsive and adapt to fit the resized window. We've used `max-width` to control the size of the image and the use of `height: auto` helps to keep the aspect ratio of the image to prevent it from looking distorted.

One might think that this is enough, right? Well no, not quite; try resizing the content to a smaller size and we can see the image is starting to spill over the border.

To make the image truly adaptive, we need to convert the sizes to their percentage equivalents; for this, we can use the formula *target ÷ context = result*. Let's put this into practice. Consider `443px` (width of image) / `800px` (original size of box) * 100 = 55.375 percent.

4. Using this formula, go ahead and modify the `img` rule as follows:

```
img { width: 55.375%; height: 37.125%; float: left; padding: 10px;
}
```

If all is well when resizing the image, the content will adjust but remain within the confines of the `#peytoe` div, as shown in this screenshot:

Peyto Lake

Peyto Lake (pea-toe) is a glacier-fed lake located in Banff National Park in the Canadian Rockies. The lake itself is easily accessed from the Icefields Parkway. It was named for Bill Peyto, an early trail guide and trapper in the Banff area.

The lake is formed in a valley of the Waputik Range, between Caldron Peak, Peyto Peak and Mount Jimmy Simpson, at an elevation of 1,860 m (6,100 ft).

During the summer, significant amounts of glacial rock flour flow into the lake, and these suspended rock particles give the lake a bright, turquoise colour. Because of its bright colour, photos of the lake often appear in illustrated books, and area around the lake is a popular sightseeing spot for tourists in the park. The lake is best seen from Bow Summit, the highest point on the Icefield Parkway.

The lake is fed by the Peyto Creek, which drains water from the Caldron Lake and Peyto Glacier (part of the Wapta Icefield), and flows into the Mistaya River..

Source: Image - Frank Kolvachok http://www.fotopedia.com/items/flickr-4110933448 (Attribution 3.0 Unported license)
Text - Wikipedia: http://en.wikipedia.org/wiki/Peyto_Lake

It should be noted that this approach may not work for all sites. For example, it may be preferable to crop it first using the background position before scaling it down to a smaller size. It will depend on your design as well as the type and quantity of images used; this is something that needs to be considered during design.

Now that we've seen the basics of making images responsive, let's move on and take a look at how we can improve on this by using higher quality images on supported devices. Before we do this though, it is worth covering a couple of key points about responsive design, namely relating to the use of vendor prefixes and image formats.

Catering to vendor prefixes and image formats

We'll start this section with a question. Hands up if you thought that creating responsive content requires special image formats or lots of vendor prefixes? If you think yes is the answer, then think again—two to three years ago, you may have had to work with something like the following lines of code as an example media query:

```
@media only screen and (-webkit-min-device-pixel-ratio: 1.5),
only screen and (min--moz-device-pixel-ratio: 1.5),
only screen and (-o-device-pixel-ratio: 3/2),
only screen and (min-device-pixel-ratio: 1.5) {
    /* High-res version of image assets go here */
}
```

Now, all you need to cater to most modern browsers (that is, versions released within the last 12 to 18 months) is this—not a vendor prefix in sight:

```
(min-resolution: 192dpi) {
    /* CSS styles here */
}
```

A similar principle applies for images—there is no need for a special format that needs to be used solely for media queries, or a need to use lots of different formats to cater to different devices. We only need to choose one format—any format will work. The exception here is that while using PNG or JPG images will produce results, you will find that the quality will begin to suffer in some instances as these formats do not scale up well.

Instead, it is better to use the SVG format when working responsively. This is effectively XML, which can be edited using tools such as Inkscape or Illustrator; it even can be edited in a text editor! The key to using SVG though is that it scales perfectly; irrespective of the size of the browser window, the image quality will be unaffected. It's an ideal format for logos, patterns, icons, and so on, but not for photographs, where the lossy format will not scale well.

Catering to different platforms

At this point, you may hopefully be asking yourself, "What about mobile devices?" — it's a good question after all: the whole point of responsive design is to cater to mobile devices! Most of the tips and tricks we will encounter throughout this chapter will work on a mobile platform, although there are some useful guidelines that are worth noting:

- Shrink the images. Use any online service such as TinyPNG or XnConvert; they need to be made as small as possible without sacrificing too much quality.

- Be careful with retina images. Memory usage for these can vary dramatically between different mobile devices, so ensure you set your media queries appropriately.

- If you're using jQuery to provide fallback support, then consider using conditional loading to only call jQuery when needed and not by default.

- Make sure that different sized versions of the same image have been created. There is no point in forcing a mobile user to download a huge file when a small one will do! To get help with this, look online for tools such as Andi Smith's Responsive Images tool at `http://www.andismith.com/grunt-responsive-images/`, which can help automate the process.

- Test in an online applet such as the Responsive tool available at `http://coolestguidesontheplanet.com/responsive/`, as there is no substitute for testing! It is much better to test thoroughly now and fix errors before going live than to suffer the embarrassment at a later date.

- Work in a mobile first capacity. Mobile devices need to be set to download the smallest images first; browsers will handle the replacement with larger images automatically if the media queries have been created within the site.

- Consider using something similar to the Network API (`http://code.tutsplus.com/tutorials/html5-network-information-api--cms-21598`) or Modernizr (`http://www.modernizr.com`) to determine whether the visitor is using a mobile platform; we can link these to jQuery/JavaScript based media queries if required to determine which image should be served.

- Don't use display: none to hide images, serve them in media queries. Using the former approach still downloads them even if they are hidden.

Remember this sentence from RevUnit's Seth Waite: "1 in 4 people abandon a web page that takes more than four seconds to load." This becomes more critical with mobile devices; loading a large image will blow this straight out of the water! You can see his original article at `http://sethwaite.com/2012/08/how-slow-website-speed-destroys-your-conversion-rates/`.

Now that the theory is out of the way, let's get coding! We're going to begin with one of the key elements of working with responsive media—catering to **high-resolution (hi-res)** or retina-based images.

Catering to HD or retina images

How often have you used a mobile device, such as an iPad, only to find images of poor quality? With the advent of retina displays on devices such as iPads, it is becoming more important to ensure your images are of sufficient quality on high-resolution screens.

Retina display is a proprietary marketing term coined by Apple, rather than a scientific term. To some it might evoke images of a complex scientific process; in reality it is just double resolution where pixels have been very closely packed to give higher quality and resolution. As an example, the pixel count can be anywhere from 220 **pixels per inch (PPI)** for third generation Mac Book Pros to 401 PPI for iPhone 6 Plus!

Adding retina support to our code is easy. There are several options open to us:

- We can set images as the background image using `background-size: cover` to ensure it covers the full display. Images can then be swapped out with higher resolution ones using CSS media queries.

- We can resize images as larger retina images then use CSS to resize them on screen; this results in a larger file but not necessarily twice as large due to the way JPEG compression works. We may need to use `-ms-interpolation-mode: bicubic` to ensure the compression level is as efficient as possible in some browsers though!

We can always set our code to display high-resolution images; however, there is a cost in displaying these images in the form of a bigger file size; the quality will be lost on **low-resolution (low-res)** devices.

Instead, we could use a plugin, such as Retina JS, to tell browsers to serve hi-res images only when needed. Let's take a look at using one in action:

1. Start by adding the following code to a new file, saving it as `retina.html`:

```
<!DOCTYPE html>
<html>
<head>
  <meta charset="utf-8">
  <script src="js/retina.min.js"></script>
</head>
<body>
```

```
    <img src="img/mothorchid.png" data-at2x="img/mothorchid@2x.png"
width="584px" height="389px">
</body>
</html>
```

2. Next, we need to download the RetinaJS library — this is available at `https://github.com/imulus/retinajs/releases/download/1.3.0/retina-1.3.0.zip` (at the time of writing of this book, the latest version is 1.3.0). Extract `retina.min.js` and drop it into a subfolder called `js` within your project folder.

3. We also need two images: one needs to be of a higher resolution than the other; for this example, I will use two PNG files that are available in the code download: `mothorchid.png` and `mothorchid@2x.png`. Note that the second file must have `@2x` at the end of the filename; this is the key to making Retina JS work.

To preview the results, it is recommended to use Google Chrome. We can easily simulate changing the device pixel ratio setting; change it from 1 to 2 and refresh the screen to see the change from the low-res image to the one of higher quality. We will cover how to create media queries that support hi-res images later in this chapter in the *Working out media queries* section.

 There are plenty of examples online of plugins that can provide retina support — two of the examples are: `responsImg`, which you can download from `http://etiennetalbot.github.io/responsImg/`. Alternatively, you can use Grunt to do the heavy work with Andi Smith's responsive images plugin for Grunt at `http://mattstow.com/experiment/responsive-images/responsive-images.html`.

Using sprites to display responsive images

So far, our examples all have something in common: they work with individual images. This is fine for those that may only appear once or twice at the most, but what if they appear frequently throughout your site? It seems pointless to have to call them each time. Fortunately, we can get around this with the use of image sprites.

 For a discussion on how image sprites work, take a look at a useful article by Chris Coyier at `http://css-tricks.com/css-sprites/`.

For the uninitiated, image sprites are a way of combining lots of (ideally, small) images into one larger one then using CSS style rules to display the relevant part of that image. We typically might use `background-position` to position the image; using values in pixels, this works perfectly well. We can use the same principle with responsive sprites but with one key difference: we use percentage values instead, not pixels! Let's take a look at how to do it using some battery icons as an example:

1. Start by extracting a copy of `imagesprites.html` from the code download that accompanies this book. It contains some simple markup with `<img>` references to some battery icons that we will use in our demo.

> At this point, you may notice the long string of random characters—these are data URIs; they were generated using the responsive sprite image creator service at `http://responsive-css.spritegen.com/`. For now, it's enough to know that these are the images converted into a format that reduces the need to continually request images from the server.

2. In a separate file, add the following code, saving it as `imagesprites.css` in the `css` subfolder of our project folder:

```css
#demo img { display: block; margin: 1em auto; }

.battery { background-position: 0 0%; background-size:
  100%; }
.battery-charge { background-position: 0 25%; background-
  size: 100%; }
.battery-full { background-position: 0 50%; background-
  size: 100%; }
.battery-half { background-position: 0 75%; background-
  size: 100%; }
.battery-plug { background-position: 0 100%; background-
  size: 100%; }

.battery, .battery-charge, .battery-full, .battery-half,
  .battery-plug
{ max-width: 100%; background-size: 100%; background-image:
  url('../img/index.png'); }
```

3. From the code download, extract a copy of `index.png` from the `img` folder. This is our sprite image that has been premade using the CSS Sprites service from earlier in this exercise. Save it in the `img` subfolder of the project folder. The battery icons used were from `http://www.fatcow.com/free-icons`. If you have others you would prefer to use, please alter the code accordingly.

4. If we preview the results, we should expect to see our responsive sprite image appear. If we resize the screen, it automatically updates the position of the image as shown in this screenshot:

However, there are some drawbacks that we need to be aware of when using this approach:

*   If we try to decode the base64 URIs given in the code, it doesn't appear to produce a valid image — what gives?
*   The use of long URIs in HTML makes it harder to read
*   It makes it very difficult, if not impossible, to adapt this code for use with `@media` queries or to use retina-based images

To see how awkward it is and to see the resulting changes in code required to remove the use of data URIs from the HTML markup, take a look at `imagesprites2.html` and `imagesprites2.css` in the code download that accompanies this book. Notice how the CSS has significantly changed.

Let's change tack — a key concept of responsive design is to determine the available viewport we can use when displaying content. Let's see what this means, when working with images.

Determining the available viewport for use

Viewport? Surely you mean screen estate or perhaps resolution? In this instance, no. When designing responsively, we have to cater to screens of all different shapes and sizes; it's not enough to simply design for a certain screen resolution. Instead, we have to allow for the fact that the available space in a browser window (or viewport) might be smaller; we have to design our breakpoints to fit this available space.

A good reference point to see the available viewport on a host of devices is `http://viewportsizes.com/` and then navigating to `http://viewportsizes.com/mine/`. This will display the current space available to us. There are two ways to set the available viewport for use: one using CSS/HTML markup and the other using jQuery or JavaScript. We'll take a look at using the CSS method first.

Using CSS to set our viewport

This is probably one of the simplest settings to add to any responsive design, yet it has the potential to open up a hornet's nest of problems! Setting the viewport using CSS is a one-line piece of code; the difficulty is in working out the CSS styling needed to position the elements correctly once the viewport has been set.

 For this demo, it is recommended that you use Google Chrome. It has a built-in device emulation facility that makes it easy to test our results in different viewports. I will assume for the purposes of this demo that you have it installed.

We'll begin with setting the markup first, so we can at least see what happens when the viewport has not been set in CSS:

1. We'll start, as always, by preparing our markup. From the code download, extract the files: `viewport-css.html`, `viewport-css.css`, and `pixel-grid. png`; save them into the `css` subfolder and `img` subfolder respectively.

2. We've used the PT Sans font for decorative purposes. This is available from `http://www.fontsquirrel.com/fonts/PT-Sans`; you will need to download it and extract the fonts into a `fonts` subfolder within your project area.

3. Open Google Chrome and set the **Emulation** facility to emulate the Sony Xperia S, Ion devices, within the Developer Toolbar.

At this point, it is worth previewing the results in a browser; if all is well, we should see a result similar to this screenshot:

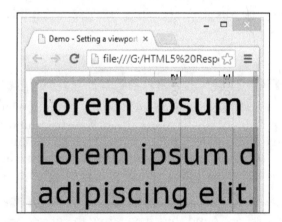

The keen-eyed among you will have noticed that something is clearly amiss. Our screen has not resized properly and text is being chopped off the right edge of the window. Let's fix that now using the following steps:

1. In `viewport-css.html`, add the following line as indicated:

   ```
   <title>Demo - Setting a viewport using CSS</title>
   <meta name="viewport" content="width=360">
   <link href="css/viewport-css.css" rel="stylesheet">
   ```

2. Resave the file and then refresh the screen in Chrome. If all is well, we can now see the results of our change with the text correctly sized and no overlap:

In this example, we've used `<meta name="viewport" content="width=360">`, which sets a very specific width of 360 px. For a more general setting where no specific width is used `<meta name="viewport" content="width=device-width, initial-scale=1">` can be set instead.

When using media queries, we can always set the size of elements within our query. It's worth setting the viewport too so that items don't disappear off the page when resizing the browser window.

> For a good discussion on using the viewport `meta` tag, it is worth checking out an article by Paul Underwood, which is available at `http://www.paulund.co.uk/understanding-the-viewport-meta-tag`.

Getting the viewport using JavaScript

The alternative to using the CSS `<meta viewport>` tag is to use JavaScript (or we could equally use jQuery). In this instance, we can work out what the values are and use these as a basis for our design, rather than simply set specific sizes as we did in the previous example.

Let's dig in and take a look to see how we can get our sizes:

1. We'll begin with adding the following markup to a new file, saving it as `viewport-js.html` in the root of our project folder:

```
<!DOCTYPE html>
<html>
<head>
  <meta charset="utf-8" />
  <title>Demo - What's my Viewport Size?</title>
  <meta name="viewport" content="width=device-width,
    initial-scale=1, minimum-scale=1, maximum-scale=1" />
  <link rel="stylesheet" href="css/viewport-js.css">
</head>
<body>
  <div id="c">
  <p>Your viewport size:</p>
  <p id="ua"></p>
  </div>
  <div id="vp"><span id="w"></span><span
    id="h"></span></div>
  <script src="js/viewport-js.js"></script>
</body>
</html>
```

2. Next, add this JavaScript to a new file, saving it as `viewport-js.js` in the `js` subfolder in the project folder:

```
(function() {
  if (typeof(document.documentElement.clientWidth) !=
    'undefined') {
    var $w = document.getElementById('w'),
        $h = document.getElementById('h'),
       $ua = document.getElementById('ua');
  $w.innerHTML = document.documentElement.clientWidth;
  $h.innerHTML = ' &times; ' +
    document.documentElement.clientHeight;
  window.onresize = function(event) {
    $w.innerHTML = document.documentElement.clientWidth;
```

```
    $h.innerHTML = ' &times; ' +
       document.documentElement.clientHeight;
  };
    $ua.innerHTML = navigator.userAgent;
  }
})();
```

3. We need some basic styling, so go ahead and add the following to viewport-js.css, saving it to the css subfolder in our project folder:

```
html, body { border: 0; margin: 0; padding: 0; font-family:
  'Helvetica',courier new; font-weight: bold; }
#vp { background: #e00; color: #fff; font-size: 3.125em;
  line-height: normal; padding: 3px; text-align: center; }
#h { color: #ff8080; }
#c { font-size: 1.25em; line-height: 1.5em; padding: 0 1em; }
```

Downloading the example code

You can download the example code files for all Packt books you have purchased from your account at http://www.packtpub.com. If you purchased this book elsewhere, you can visit http://www.packtpub.com/support and register to have the files e-mailed directly to you.

4. If we preview the results in a browser, we'll see the size of our available viewport area displayed along with the current user agent string being used by our browser, as shown in this screenshot:

Your viewport size:

Mozilla/5.0 (Windows NT 6.3; WOW64; rv:31.0) Gecko/20100101 Firefox/31.0

910 × 460

There are plenty of good examples online to show us how to determine the available viewport area; we've used a modified version of one produced by Matt Stow at http://viewportsizes.com/. In it, he also has an extensive list of viewport sizes for a variety of devices. We could of course use something like Modernizr to perform the same function, but this is at the expense of depending on an outside solution; our example here is written in vanilla JavaScript, removing any dependencies and keeping the code concise.

Working out media queries

Now that we've worked out how much space we have to work with, we can now work out what happens to elements when we hit the limits of our available space. This is particularly relevant if we want to display hi-res images for example. After all, we don't want to show a high quality image if it chokes the available bandwidth of our device!

Let's take a look at how we can use media queries to switch between lo-res and hi-res versions of a single image:

1. We will start with setting up the markup we need for our demo. From the code bundle for this book, extract a copy of `min-resolution.html` and save it to the root of the project folder.

2. In a new file, add these style rules and save it as `min-resolution.css` in the `css` subfolder of our project folder. This is where the magic happens, that is, switching from the lo-res to hi-res versions of our image:

```css
#orchid { background-image: url('../img/mothorchid.png');
   height: 24.31rem; width: 36.5rem; }


@media (min-resolution: 120dpi) {
   #orchid { background-image:
     url('../img/mothorchid@2x.png');
       height: 24.31rem; width: 36.5rem; }
}
```

3. From the code download that accompanies this book, extract and save copies of `mothorchid.png` and `mothorchid@2x.png` into the `img` subfolder of our project folder.

4. If we preview the results of our work, we will first see the standard resolution image `mothorchid.png`.

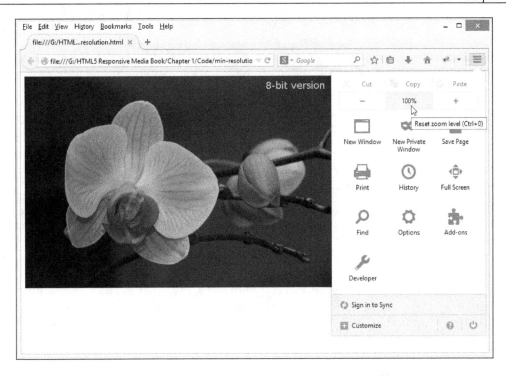

5. However, if we resize the image by zooming in to at least 133 percent, we will see it switch to its hi-res equivalent.

6. Click on the – button to reset back to 100 percent and we will see the image revert back to the standard resolution version.

Using Google Chrome?

We can achieve the same effect using Chrome's Developer Toolbar. Press *Ctrl + Shift + I* to display it and then click on the drawer icon. Now, switch to the **Screen** tab and change the Device pixel ratio setting from 1 to 2 to show the hi-res image. For more details, please visit `https://developer.chrome.com/devtools/docs/device-mode`.

At this point, we can use this trick to display any hi-res image we need; the key is to ensure we have two images, one of a standard resolution, while the other is of a higher quality. A small word of note though—if you spend any time researching different types of media queries, then you may come across something akin to these lines of code:

```
@media (-webkit-min-device-pixel-ratio: 1.25),
(min-resolution: 120dpi){
    /* Retina-specific stuff here */
}
```

While still perfectly usable, the initial `-webkit-min-device-pixel-ratio` setting has been deprecated in favor of min-resolution; there is no need to use it unless you have to cater to really old browsers!

Now, we could easily use CSS queries in all of our projects, but there may still be occasions where standard queries might not work. A good example is for a navigation that behaves differently at different sizes. Fortunately, there is a solution for this—we can achieve a similar effect using the `breakpoints.js` library. Let's delve in now and take a look.

Using pure JS to determine page breakpoints

So far, we've worked mainly with modern browsers. These handle media queries effectively, allowing us to display the right image at the right time. What if we had to support old IE browsers, for example, that can't handle media queries without some form of help? No problem—enter `breakpoints.js`, one of the many JavaScript/jQuery libraries available to help us mimic media queries. I feel an exercise coming on, so let's make a start building an example to see how it works:

1. We'll begin with setting up our markup for the demo. This contains some simple textboxes set to show in a group. For this, we need to extract copies of `breakpoints.html` and `breakpoints.css` from the code download that accompanies this book. Save them both into the project folder: the HTML file at the root and the CSS file within the `css` subfolder.

2. We need a copy of jQuery 2.x—there should already be one in our project folder from earlier demos; if not, extract a copy from the code download that accompanies this book or from `http://code.jquery.com`.

Although `breakpoints.js` is a few years old, I've tested it with jQuery 2.1.1 with no noticeable issues seen.

3. Next comes the all important `breakpoints.js` library. Go ahead and extract a copy from the code download that accompanies this book and save it to the `js` subfolder of our project folder. Newer versions will be available at `http://xoxco.com/projects/code/breakpoints/`.

4. We need to add the call to initialize our breakpoints, so go ahead and add this code in between the empty `<script>` tags:

```
$(function () {
  $.breakpoints({
    '.article': {
      'small': [0, 320],
      'medium': [320, 480],
      'large': [480, null]
    }
  });
});
```

5. Save your work. If all is well, we should see these three boxes when previewing our work in a browser session:

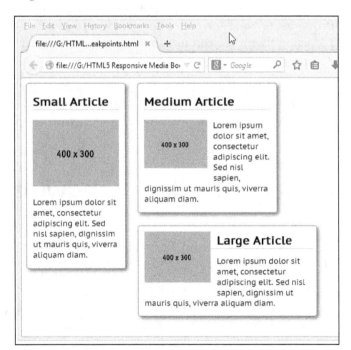

At this point, try resizing the browser window. Notice how each of the text boxes resize. We're using image placeholders from the Placehold.it service at `http://placehold.it/`; these automatically resize in the same manner.

> There is a working example of this exercise available on the code download for this book — extract `breakpoints-finished.html` and `breakpoints-finished.css`, along with jQuery and `breakpoints.js`, then rename the HTML and CSS files to `breakpoints.html` and `breakpoints.css` to view the demo. You will need to store them in the appropriate subfolder of our project folder for them to work correctly.

But hold on! A closer look at the CSS shows no media queries. This is the beauty of `breakpoints.js`; it allows us to replicate media queries for those browsers that don't support them natively. Sure, it's a little extra overhead; we can get around this using conditional comments (or Modernizr), so the overhead only appears when needed.

> There are other examples available online that you may prefer to use. Take a look at `http://www.responsivejs.com` or search through GitHub to find alternatives.

Let's move forward and take a look at a different method of switching images; so far we've used media queries to handle which image should be displayed. However, we're not limited to using them. We can use an alternative method in the form of source shuffling.

Source shuffling uses both jQuery and CSS — if JavaScript is disabled, then CSS media queries will kick in and perform a similar function instead. Let's dig into an example to see how it works and why this could potentially provide the best of both solutions to us.

Using data tags to allow bandwidth constraints

The title of this exercise is a real mouthful, but serves to highlight an interesting experiment: "What if we could use data tags to switch images?"

The immediate benefit of source shuffling is that it keeps CSS media queries out of the HTML markup (to see what I mean, take a look at the HTML code used in *Working with the <picture> tags* in the next section.)

It's an interesting concept and one you may want to consider using; to see how it works, we'll use an adapted version of an example created by the UX designer Jordan Moore. This uses JavaScript-based Conditional CSS library by Jeremy Keith to great effect. To see what I mean, let's get going on a demo to see how it works:

1. Our journey through this demo starts with setting up the markup needed. In a new file, add the following and save it as `datatags.html` in the root of our project area:

```html
<!DOCTYPE html>
<html>
  <head>
    <title>Responsive Images using data- tags - Demo</title>
    <meta charset="utf-8" />
    <meta name="viewport" content="width=device-width,initial-
      scale=1">
    <link rel="stylesheet" href="css/datatags.css">
    <script src="js/jquery.min.js"></script>
    <script src="js/onmediaquery.min.js"></script>
    <script src="js/datatags.js"></script>
  </head>
  <body>
    <img class="thumbnail" src="img/small.jpg" data-
      medium="img/ medium.jpg" data-large="img/large.jpg"
      alt="Responsive images example">
  </body>
</html>
```

2. We now need a handful of accompanying files. From the code bundle, extract `small.jpg`, `medium.jpg`, and `large.jpg` and save these to the `img` subfolder in our project folder.

3. Next comes the three JavaScript files that we need: `jquery.min.js`, `onmediaquery.min.js`, and `datatags.js` should be extracted from the code download and saved into the `js` subfolder of our project area.

4. Finally, we need some styling. In a new file, add the following and save it as `datatags.css` in our `css` subfolder:

```css
img { max-width: 100%; }
body:after { content: "global"; display: none; }

@media screen and (min-width: 35em) {
  body:after { content: "tablet"; display: none; }
}

@media screen and (min-width: 56em) {
  body:after { content: "desktop"; display: none; }
}
```

5. We're all set. If all is well, we should see our small image appear first followed immediately by either of the large ones, depending on the size of our browser window.

The key to note in this demo is that we will only see the `small.jpg` image on mobile devices where the viewport is already smaller. On larger devices and desktops, either the `medium.jpg` or `large.jpg` images will be shown instead as dictated by the media query in effect.

Working with the <picture> tags

When working in responsive design, we frequently have to provide different images and use a series of media queries to display the right ones at the appropriate time. This works fine, but is a little labor intensive. Instead, we can use the upcoming `<picture>` tag to produce a neater effect.

 Support for the `<picture>` tag is still somewhat early; we have to use a polyfill to provide support for the tag for some browsers. For more details, it's worth checking the CanIUse.com site at `http://caniuse.com/#feat=picture`.

Let's dive in and take a look at how we can use the tag using these steps:

1. We'll start, as always, with setting up the markup for our demo. From the code download that accompanies this book, extract copies of the `picturefill.html`, `picturefill.css`, and `picturefill.js` files; save these into the root, `css`, and `js` subfolders of our project area, respectively.

2. In the code download, there are three images we also need: `small.jpg`, `medium.jpg`, and `large.jpg`; these need to go into the `img` subfolder as well.

Now, we have our demo set up. Next, try resizing the browser window smaller or larger. Notice how the two images change, albeit at different response points. The key to this is the use of the `picturefill.js` polyfill created by Scott Jehl. This aims to replicate the functionality of `<picture>` until such time as the browser supports it natively and we can remove the fall back.

The library is called using this script block—`document.createElement` is used to create a dummy `picture` fallback element, as it doesn't exist yet at this point:

```
<script>
  document.createElement( "picture" );
</script>
<script async="true" src="js/picturefill.js"></script>
```

We then provide the fallback code as follows:

```
<p>Here's how that renders in the browser. Feel free to resize
    to see it change.</p>
<img sizes="(min-width: 20em) 80vw, 100vw" srcset="img/small.jpg
    375w, img/medium.jpg 480w, img/large.jpg 768w" alt="A random
    image">
```

This is followed by the native <picture> element, which will be supported by Firefox, Opera, and Chrome within the next few versions of each browser:

```
<picture>
    <source srcset="img/large.jpg" media="(min-width: 768px)">
    <source srcset="img/medium.jpg" media="(min-width: 480px)">
    <img srcset="img/small.jpg" media="(min-width: 375px)">
</picture>
```

It's worth getting to know the <picture> element. While it means that we have to have our CSS media queries in-line, it produces a cleaner result as we don't need to use individual media queries in a separate style sheet.

 Rather than using plain PNG or JPG images, you may like to look at using WebP images instead. They are technically similar but provide a better compression rate. You may need to get additional support added to use them in applications such as GIMP (visit http://registry.gimp.org/node/25874).

Maintaining the <picture> tag in our code

A small word of warning: the <picture> tag is still very new, so expect there to be changes to the overall design before it is finalized. It may raise some important questions about whether using it is right for your needs and how it should be maintained within your code; for example, are you happy to use it, but accept that not every browser might support it yet? Are your needs such that you can't use it yet, but can live with using a polyfill as an interim measure?

If you do decide to use it, it will require careful planning in terms of implementing it. Thankfully, Scott Jehl's implementation (as used in this chapter), is close to the intended final version of <picture>; this should make the switchover relatively painless.

 To get an up-to-date picture (pun intended!) of the latest state of play with the <picture> tag and its use for responsive images, it's worth taking a look at the Responsive Image Community Group's site at http://responsiveimages.org/.

In the last exercise, we mentioned some different formats and that something similar to WebP is a better alternative; we can do even better by using SVG, when working responsively. How? Let me reveal all with a look at using it for improved scalability.

Working with the SVG image format for scalability

If you have spent any time working with media in a responsive capacity, no doubt you will find that some image formats don't resize well. To get around it, it may be necessary to provide several different versions of our image and set the code to pick the right one at the appropriate point.

Do we want to be doing that all the time? Somehow I don't think so. It's a real pain to produce all those different versions! There's a better way to achieve the same result if we switch to using the vector-based SVG format, which will resize smoothly without loss of quality. Let's delve into an example to see how it works:

1. We'll start with preparing the images that we will use for the purposes of this demo. We'll use the dark modern LCD display SVG image that is available from the XOO.me website at `http://xoo.me/template/details/12636-dark-modern-lcd-display-vector`. If you prefer to use an alternative, then please alter the code accordingly; we will need PNG and SVG versions of the same image.

2. Add this code to a new file and save it as `svgfallback.html` in the root of our project folder:

```
<!DOCTYPE html>
<html>
<head>
  <meta charset="utf-8">
  <link rel="stylesheet" href="css/svgfallback.css">
</head>
<body>
  This is an image displayed using SVG, with PNG fallback:
  <br>
  <div id="lcd"></div>
</body>
</html>
```

3. Next, add the following CSS styles to a new file and save it as `svgfallback.css` in the `css` subfolder of our project folder:

```
#lcd { background: url('../img/lcd.png');
  background-image: url('../img/lcd.svg'), none;
  width: 576px; height: 383px; background-repeat: no-repeat; }
```

4. Let's see what happens when we preview the results in most browsers; it will show the SVG image of our LCD monitor. Let's first look at the source code of our page in a DOM inspector where we can see both PNG and SVG ticked as shown in this screenshot; the latter takes precedence:

```
    }
  ◢#lcd  {                              svgfallback.css (1)
    ☑ background:   ▷ url('../img/lcd.png');
    ☑ background-image:  url('../img/lcd.svg'), none;
    ☑ width:  576px;
    ☑ height:  383px;
    ☑ background-repeat:  no-repeat;

    }
```

5. To prove it works, the following is the SVG image in all its glory:

This is an image displayed using SVG, with PNG fallback:

6. To force our demo to display the PNG fallback, we need to emulate a browser that doesn't support SVG images natively; IE8 is a perfect candidate for this. I recommend using a recent version of IE, such as 9 or 10. We can use its Emulation mode to force it to display in IE8 mode, and therefore choose the PNG image instead:

```
⊿#lcd  {                                    svgfallback.css (1)
  ☑ background:   ▷ url(../img/lcd.png);
     background-image: url('../img/lcd.svg'), none;
  ☑ width: 576px;
  ☑ height: 383px;
  ☑ background-repeat: no-repeat;
}
```

The beauty of using SVG is that we can actually edit the content of the image using a text editor; SVG images are after all just plain XML files! SVG images are great for several reasons:

- They are small file sizes that compress well
- They scale to any size without losing clarity (except very tiny)
- They look great on retina display
- They design control like interactivity and filters

Using standard images such as PNGs or JPGs will work, but they won't resize properly beyond their native resolution; instead, we are likely to need several versions of the same image in order to view them properly. It's worth spending time getting to know the SVG format. There is a useful article by Nick Salloum at `http://callmenick.com/2014/04/02/svg-fallback-with-png/`, which extols different mechanisms we can use to provide fallback for SVG images.

If you really want to get into editing SVG images, take a look at `http://css-tricks.com/using-svg/`. It's a great article by Chris Coyier that shows us how we can edit the content to really alter its appearance.

Using image icons for scalability

One of the major problems we have when creating responsive content is the use of icons: their bitmap format doesn't scale well when resizing them. This is often the same for icon sprites; for example, if you resize the battery icons demo from earlier in the chapter, then you will soon notice how pixelated it becomes when anti-aliasing kicks in!

To get around this, designers may simply drop the use of icons; the alternative is to replace them with vector-based web fonts, such as the Font Awesome icons, available at `http://fortawesome.github.io/Font-Awesome/`. There is an excellent article online by Jason Cranford Teague at `http://webstandardssherpa.com/reviews/responsive-webfont-icons`, extolling the benefits of using them in the main due to their scalability with no loss of fidelity.

To see how they work in action, we're going to use some social media icons from Entypo, created by Daniel Bruce and available at `http://www.entypo.com`. For this tutorial, we're going to use a simplified version of an example created by Teague, which uses a number of icons. You can see the original article at `http://webstandardssherpa.com/reviews/responsive-webfont-icons`.

Perform these steps for this tutorial:

1. Let's start by extracting a copy of `webicons.html` and `webicons.css` from the code download that accompanies this book. Instead of building this up (particularly as it uses a fair bit of CSS), we're going to take a look at some of the key concepts in use. Store the `webicons.css` file in the `css` subfolder of our project folder, while the `webicons.html` file should be stored at the root.

2. If we preview the file in a browser window, we will see a range of icons displayed; the screenshot shows them resized in Firefox at 67 percent:

3. Try zooming in and out. Notice how the icons increase and decrease in size without any apparent loss of quality? We've used web fonts, in place of standard images; this principle works beautifully for simple icons such as the logos used in our example. The key to this is the use of the `rem` sizes or root `em`. This sizes each character to the font size of the HTML element not the parent, which is used by `em`.

There's a useful article by Jonathan Snook that explains how `rem` and `em` work, available at `http://snook.ca/archives/html_and_css/font-size-with-rem`.

4. Notice the use of the format set for each icon? This is the **Unicode Private Use** area of the font; instead of using t from the font (which represents the Twitter icon), we can use this private use area. It achieves the same result. The only difference being that the letter t is not displayed when using the private area.

 For more information about Unicode Private Use Areas, take a look at the article on Wikipedia at http://en.wikipedia. org/wiki/Private_Use_Areas.

Let's move on and take a look at a couple of examples of real-world applications of responsive design, beginning with *Building a responsive carousel*.

Building a responsive carousel

So far we've covered a lot of different techniques to help us produce responsive content. Most of it has been simple examples in a development context. It's time to take a look at a couple of examples of real-world applications where responsive functionality has been put to good use. Our first example is in the form of a responsive carousel. There are dozens of example libraries online that can be used to create one, so there is no need to build from scratch!

Let's take a look at one of my favorites — ResponsiveSlides.js; it's a simple library that provides a useful solution, but doesn't try to achieve everything. We'll borrow one of their examples to see how it works.

1. As always, we need to start somewhere. Let's begin by downloading the ResponsiveSlides library from http://responsiveslides.com/; the current version is 1.5.4 at the time of writing. Save this in the js subfolder of our project folder.

2. We also need the styling file for ResponsiveSlides, along with a copy of the jQuery library. Extract a copy of carousel.css, saving it in the css subfolder of our project folder; then do the same for jQuery in the js subfolder.

 The ResponsiveSlides package comes with jQuery 1.8.3; I've tested it with Version 2.1.1 of jQuery with no apparent ill effects.

3. Next, extract a copy of carousel.html from the code download that accompanies this book; add the following code between the empty <script> tags immediately below the link to the responsiveslides.js library:

```
<script>
  $(function () {
```

```
    $("#slides1").responsiveSlides({ auto: false, pagination:
true, nav: true, fade: 500, maxwidth: 800
     });
   });
<script>
```

4. Save the file. If we preview the results in a browser, we will see our carousel appear.

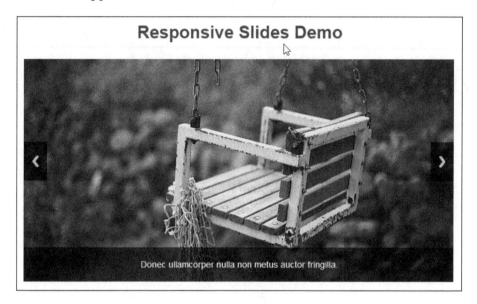

5. Try resizing the browser window now. We should see the carousel reduce in size but continue to scroll through the images with no loss of quality.

There are plenty of examples of responsive carousels available online—two such examples are WOW Slider at `http://wowslider.com/`, with an example of what is possible at `http://www.wowslider.com/responsive-image-gallery-glass-collage.html`, Owl Carousel (`http://www.owlgraphic.com/owlcarousel`) and BXSlider, available at `http://bxslider.com/`. It is a matter of trying a selection and choosing the one that suits your requirements.

There is a prebuilt working example on the code download that accompanies this book. Extract copies of `carousel-finished.html` and `carousel-finished.css`, then rename them to `carousel.html` and `carousel.css`. You will need to extract the accompanying libraries, as outlined in this exercise, for it to operate correctly.

Creating responsive maps using Google Maps

In the second of our two real-world examples, we're going to look at making a responsive map using Google Maps. Responsive maps, I hear you ask? Surely this should come automatically, right? Well no, it doesn't, which makes its use a little awkward on mobile devices. Fortunately, we can easily fix this; the great thing about it is that it only requires a little additional CSS:

1. Let's make a start by browsing to `http://maps.google.com`, then entering the zip code of our chosen location. In this instance, I will use the UK office of Packt Publishing, which is B3 2PB.

2. Click on the cog, then select **Share and embed map**:

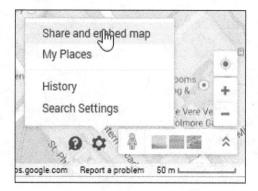

3. In the dialog box that appears, switch to the **Embed map** tab, then copy the contents of the text field starting with `<iframe src=`....

4. In a copy of the code download that accompanies this book, extract a copy of `googlemaps.html` in your favorite text editor and add the `<iframe>` code in between the `google-maps div` tags.

5. Next, add this CSS styling to a new file and save it as `googlemaps.css`:

```
#container { margin: 0 auto; padding: 5px; max-width:
  40rem; }
.google-maps { position: relative; padding-bottom: 60%;
  height: 0; overflow: hidden; }
.google-maps iframe { position: absolute; top: 0; left: 0;
  width: 100% !important; height: 100% !important; }
```

If all is well, we will see a Google Maps image of Birmingham with our office marked accordingly:

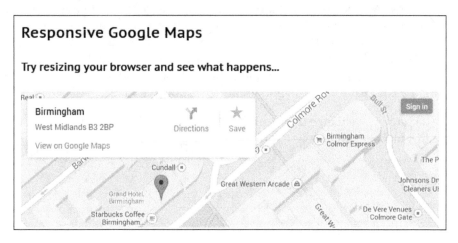

At this point, try resizing the browser window. You will see that the map resizes automatically; the CSS styling that we've added has overridden the standard styles used within Google Maps to make our map responsive and accessible from any device we care to use.

Summary

Wow! We've certainly covered a lot over the last few pages! Let's take a moment to recap and let what we've learned sink in.

We began with a look at creating basic fluid images, which are a key to responsive design and should form the mainstay for any responsively designed site. We then covered some key points in the form of what image formats to use, as well as whether we need to use any vendor prefixes in our code. Next up came a discussion on some useful tips to cater to mobile devices. We saw how many are common sense, but particularly apply when designing for mobile devices.

Our first coding example came in the form of a look at catering to high-definition or retina images; we then moved on to examining how we can also use sprites to add responsive media to our projects. We then moved on to looking at sizing our available viewport space using both jQuery and CSS; these we can then use to determine what our media queries should look like. We also covered off how you can use JavaScript to define media queries as well, in the event we need to provide fallback support in our sites.

Moving on, next up we covered a couple of examples of how to switch images responsively—the first using data tags and the second using the upcoming `<picture>` tags. We also looked at a trick whereby we can provide two images at the same time but rely on the browser to pick which one it can support. We finished our look at using images in the form of a peek at how we can use web icons to serve content responsively and that these scale beautifully without any loss of quality. We then finished of the chapter with a look at two real-world examples in the form of building a responsive carousel and creating responsive maps.

In the next chapter, we'll take a look at the other major element of media content and how to add videos responsively to our sites.

2
Adding Responsive Video Content

Throughout the history of the Internet, since its early days, designers and developers have been able to add images to websites — these are great to illustrate points or concepts, but are a static record at a point in time. More and more developers are turning to the power of video to help illustrate something: the themes are varied, from news right through to cooking, or even a step-by-step coding tutorial! With the advent of mobile media comes an increasing need for responsive content — we need to ensure our content can be viewed without issue on more and more devices.

In this chapter, we'll go on a journey through some of the concepts required to make our content responsive, as well as cover some of the tips and tricks to make our content available on multiple platforms. In this chapter, we will cover the following topics:

- Determining support for the `<video>` formats and choosing the right format
- Embedding HTML5 video content
- Determining an available viewport for use
- Catering to fallback support and applying vendor fixes
- Using JavaScript libraries to provide support
- Catering to different platforms and displaying full size videos

Curious? Let's get started!

We will begin with the basics of choosing the right format for HTML5 video, but first, we need to cover some simple administrative tasks that will help us throughout the chapter.

Getting ready

For the purpose of our exercises in this chapter, we'll be using similar markup throughout; it is worth saving the following code as a template file to help you complete each exercise:

```
<!DOCTYPE html>
<html>
<head>
  <meta charset="utf-8"/>
  <title>XXXXXXXXXX</title>
  <meta name="viewport" content="width=device-width, minimum-
    scale=1.0, maximum-scale=1.0" />
  <link href="css/XXXXXXXX.css" rel="stylesheet">
</head>
<body>
</body>
</html>
```

Now that we have our groundwork prepared, let's begin our journey into working with responsive video, with a look first at the formats available for use.

We will also be using various videos from the Big Buck Bunny Project by the Blender Foundation, namely the 852 x 480 and 1280 x 720 formats; you can download these from `http://www.bigbuckbunny.org/index.php/download/`.

> The videos used throughout this project are copyright © 2008, Blender Foundation, available at `www.bigbuckbunny.org`.

It is also recommended that you create a project folder for the purposes of this chapter; I called mine `code`. Inside it, you will need to create two folders: `css` and `js`. We will refer to these two folders throughout the chapter.

Determining support for <video> formats

The first step on our journey in creating responsive video content is to determine which video format we're going to use. There are several video formats available for use in the browser, but the two worth noting are WebM and MP4. The former is still supported within Firefox, Chrome, and Opera only; the latter is supported by all of the main desktop browsers, except IE8 and Opera. For the purposes of creating responsive content, we still need to work with both though, as the mobile platform has yet to decide on a common standard:

Browser	Firefox	Chrome	Safari	IE (9+)	Opera	iOS	Android
Format supported	MP4	MP4	MP4	MP4	WebM	MP4, WebM	MP4, WebM

This table can also be referred to at `http://www.jwplayer.com/html5/` (in the article "The State of HTML5 Video", by Jeroen Wijering).

As the HTML5 video standard is still in something of a state of flux, it is worth checking the CanIUse.com site, to keep abreast of progress at `http://caniuse.com/#search=video`.

 You may come across references to the OGG format as an HTML5 <video> standard; while this will work perfectly well, the format was removed from the HTML5 standard in 2007, due to issues with patents. It is not as widely supported as the other formats.

Now that we're up to speed on video formats, let's take a look at getting our video content converted to the right format, ready for use.

Choosing the right format

So far, we've learnt that to work with the HTML5 <video> tags, we need to use either the WebM or MP4 formats (or ideally both, to ensure coverage). It's possible that you may have existing content that isn't in this format; if this is the case, let's look at how we can get it converted.

There are dozens of applications available for download, to convert from one format to another — my personal favorite is XMedia Recode for Windows, which is available at `http://www.xmedia-recode.de`. This allows conversion to and from a host of different formats, including both WebM and MP4. Let's take a look at how it works using the following steps:

1. We'll start by downloading a copy of XMedia Recode from `http://www.xmedia-recode.de/en/download.html`; the latest version is 3.1.9.4 at the time of this writing.

2. Double-click on the setup executable to launch installation and accept all defaults throughout the wizard.

    At this point, XMedia Recode will be installed; we now need to run through the conversion process. It's possible to really go to town on configuring the conversion process — for now, we'll stick to the basic conversion, which is sufficient for our needs.

3. In the XMedia Recode application, click on **Open File**, then select your video and click on **Open**.

4. Wait for XMedia Recode to analyze the video, and then select the desired format from the **Output Format** box.

5. At the foot of the window, we need to select our destination folder, so go ahead and select the same folder where you store your video content.

We're about ready to begin the conversion; to do so, we need to click on **Add to queue** and then on **Encode** to start the process, as shown in the following screenshot:

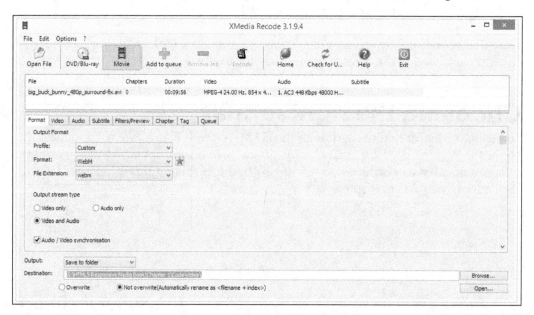

XMedia Recode will prompt when the conversion process is completed. We can either elect to convert another video or close the application at this point. For those of us who use Apple Macs or Linux, there are several alternatives available; they perform a similar process to XMedia Recode. A couple of options that are worth looking at are the cross-platform application Handbrake (`http://www.handbrake.fr`— for MP4 conversion), and the browser-based Firefogg applet available at `http://www.firefogg.org`. Although the latter is meant to convert to OGG format, it will also convert videos to WebM format as well.

> For more information on the WebM format, or if you have any difficulty in configuring it for use on your PC, then take a look at the documentation for the project at `http://www.webmproject.org/tools`.

We now have our videos ready, so what's next? Ah yes—let's take a look at embedding them into a page, so we can see how to make them responsive. We'll use some converted videos from the Big Buck Bunny Project as our source media; if you would like to try something smaller, there are sample videos available at `http://techslides.com/sample-webm-ogg-and-mp4-video-files-for-html5/`, which will work equally well.

Embedding HTML5 video content

As with all projects, we need to start somewhere—we could simply double-click on a video and let it play in any application we have installed, that supports the format. However, this isn't what we're here to do; we want to view the content in a browser and set it to resize automatically!

The following steps will show you how to achieve this using videos I've converted from the open source Big Bunny Project at `http://www.bigbuckbunny.org`:

1. Let's start by opening a copy of the template file we created earlier in the book, then alter the `<title>` tag of our demo, as shown in the following code snippet:

    ```
    <title>Demo: Controlling Video sizes using media queries</title>
    ```

2. In the `<body>` tag of our code, go ahead and add the following lines; these reference the different video formats we can use, depending on which browser we're working with:

    ```
    <video controls>
      <source src="video/bigbuckbunny.mp4" type="video/mp4">
    ```

```
        <source src="video/bigbuckbunny.webm"
          type="video/webm">
    </video>
```

Save the results as `basic.html`. At this point, if we were to preview the results in a browser, we can clearly see that we have a problem! The video hasn't resized, resulting in only part of it being displayed:

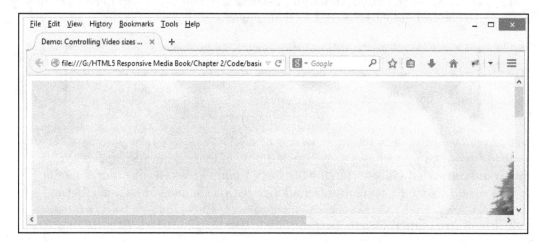

3. Fortunately, it's easy to fix; if you were expecting a lot of complicated CSS code, then fear not; the solution is easier than you think! Add the following to a new file, saving it as `basic.css`:

```css
video {
    max-width: 100%;
    width: 100% !important;
    /* just in case, to force correct aspect ratio */
    height: auto !important;
}
```

4. In `basic.html`, go ahead and amend the CSS style sheet link as shown here:

```html
<link href="css/basic.css" rel="stylesheet"></head>
```

If we refresh our browser, we can now see that the content is responsive, resizing automatically when we reduce the browser window in size:

Now that our initial content is set up and working, we need to consider one important point—what if we're designing for a small viewport? Should we still display the video or hide it on smaller devices such as mobile phones? All these questions are good ones. Let's take a look at how we can determine our available viewport size so we can decide what will or will not be included in our design.

If you find that videos don't play correctly, then you may need to create a `.htaccess` file at the root of your project folder, then add the following lines of code in that file:

```
AddType video/mp4 mp4
AddType video/ogg ogv
AddType video/webm webm
```

Determining an available viewport for use

If you have spent any time developing content for responsive layouts, you will have no doubt come across media queries. The same applied to videos; you could typically see something akin to the following (simplified) example:

```
<video controls>
  <source src="the-sky-is-calling-large.mp4" media="screen and
    (min-width:800px)">
  <source src="the-sky-is-calling-small.mp4" media="screen and
    (max-width:799px)">
</video>
```

Unfortunately, most browsers have since removed support for media queries. This is largely due to the poor user experience we get if the video is suddenly interrupted when resizing the screen. Fortunately, we can produce similar effects, although we need to resort to JavaScript or jQuery to achieve this. In this next example, we're going to show a small video if the screen is resized to a small window, or hide it when displayed in full screen. Let's take a look at how we can achieve this:

1. We'll begin with extracting a copy of `viewport.html`, along with the `video`, `js`, and `css` folders from the code download that accompanies this book.

2. Next comes the real magic behind this demo. In the `js` folder is a copy of `detect.js`; this controls the display of our video according to the size of the available viewport. Let's go through it in sections, starting with the creation of the `wi` variable, to store the current window size:

   ```
   $(window).ready(function() {
     var wi = $(window).width();
   ```

3. Next comes the rendering of the initial size of our window using the following line of code:

   ```
   $("p.notification").text('Initial screen width is
     currently: ' + wi + 'px.');
   ```

4. The real magic happens next. In the resize function, we get the new width, then work out if we're below `480px` and set the video to display if `true`:

   ```
   $(window).resize(function() {
     var wi = $(window).width();

     var video = $("#video").html();

     if (wi <= 480){
       $("p.notification").text('Screen width is less than
         or equal to 480px. Width is currently: ' + wi +
         'px.');
   ```

```
if (video == "") {
  $("#video").append('<video controls><source
    src="video/bigbuckbunny-320px.mp4"
    type="video/mp4"></video>');
  }
}
```

5. If the size is larger, then the video is hidden:

```
else {
  $("p.notification").text('Screen width is greater than
480px. Width is currently: ' + wi + 'px.');
  $("#video").html("");
  }
});
});
```

6. Now, let's run the demo in a browser to see the results. If we try resizing the browser window to below `480px`, we should see a notification appear, along with the video, as shown in the following screenshot:

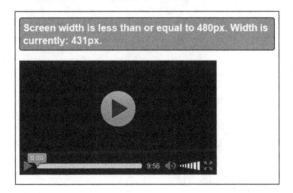

7. Try resizing the window to a larger size. Notice how the video is no longer displayed.

Although this demo is somewhat simplistic in nature, it shows that we can mimic the effects of media queries. So, we can work out what space is available to us and either display a larger, high-quality video, or one of a smaller size. After all, we don't want to download a huge video on a mobile when a smaller version is available!

> **How can I see the effects of resizing my browser window?**
>
> We could always resize it manually, but a better solution is to use a resizer tool such as the one created by Malte Wasserman, which simulates a range of sizes and is available at `http://lab.maltewassermann.com/viewport-resizer/`.

The example does open up some possibilities, although it should be handled with care, and any solution you develop needs to be fully tested before being implemented in production.

Catering to fallback support

So far, we've produced HTML5-formatted video content and seen how to embed it in our pages. There may be occasions, though, when we are working on a device that doesn't support a certain type of video format.

While support for HTML5 video is improving all the time, we're still at a stage where not every platform supports the same formats. This leaves us with two choices. We can either try to incorporate a different format, or we can simply set the content to degrade gracefully. We've looked at providing different formats, so let's switch track and see how we can gracefully degrade our content using Modernizr as the basis for our test. The following steps will guide us through the process of content degrading:

1. Let's begin by adding the following code to a new file and save it as `modernizr.html`:

```
<!DOCTYPE html>
<html class="no-js">
<head>
  <meta charset="utf-8"/>
  <title> Demo: Detecting support with Modernizr</title>
  <meta name="viewport" content="width=device-width,
    minimum-scale=1.0, maximum-scale=1.0" />
  <link rel="stylesheet" href="css/modernizr.css">
  <script src="js/jquery.js"></script>
  <script src="js/modernizr.min.js"></script>
  <script>
    $(document).ready(function() {
      if(Modernizr.video) {
        $("#html5video").html("");
        var videoHTML = '<video controls><source
          src="video/bigbuckbunny.mp4"
          type="video/mp4"><source
          src="video/bigbuckbunny.webm"
          type="video/webm"></video>';
        $("#html5video").html(videoHTML);
      }
    });
  </script>
</head>
<body>
```

```
<div id="html5video">Sorry, HTML5 video is not enabled on
   this client</div>
</body>
</html>
```

2. Next, add the following code to a new file and save it as `modernizr.css`. This will provide some basic styling in the event that the video test proves negative:

```
video { width: 50%; }
.no-js #html5video { background-color: #c00; color: #fff;
   font-weight: bold; font-family: arial, helvetica; font-
   size: 14px; border: 2px solid black; border-radius: 4px;
   width: 35%; padding: 10px; }
```

3. We need to provide some additional files. From the code download that accompanies this book, extract the `js` and `video` folders; save these in the project folder.

4. To test this, we'll use Firefox; in the browser address bar, enter `about:config` to bring up the configuration settings.

5. Click on **I'll be careful, I promise!** in the security warning message that pops up. Then look for **javascript.enabled** and double-click on it to set it to **false**:

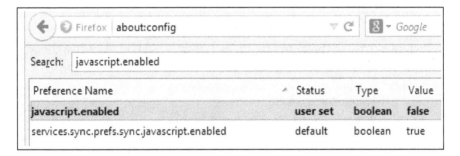

At this point, let's preview the results of our effort in the browser. If all is well, we should not see our video, but the following warning instead:

6. Return to step 5, but this time double-click on the entry to enable JavaScript support. Once done, refresh the preview, where we should see our all too familiar Buck Bunny video.

Now, what happens if our video content can't be converted to HTML5 format for some reason? A good example might be that the content is only available in YouTube or Vimeo format; copyright restrictions may prevent us from converting it. It's not a problem though; we can still use it. While it is strictly speaking not going to be in HTML5 format, we can still make it responsive with a little additional effort.

Using JS libraries to provide support

One of the key benefits of using the HTML5 <video> element is that resizing is a breeze; it only takes a couple of lines of CSS to make videos responsive when using this tag. However, the same cannot be said for videos of other formats; we may come across occasions when we are forced to use formats such as YouTube or Vimeo, which rely on embedding through the use of <iframes>.

Thankfully, we can make these responsive although the route to doing so is a little more involved. It requires the use of a library such as FitVids.js, available at http://www.fitvidsjs.com, which works with jQuery. The following steps will help us use JS libraries to make the videos responsive:

1. We'll start by first downloading the FitVids library. Browse to https://github.com/davatron5000/FitVids.js, then click on **Download ZIP** on the right. From the archive, extract and save jquery.fitvids.js into your project folder.

2. Next, in a copy of the template file we created earlier, alter the <head> section as shown in the following code snippet:

```
<head>
  <meta charset="utf-8">
  <title>Demo - Using FitVids.js</title>
  <script src="js/jquery.js"></script>
  <script src="js/jquery.fitvids.js"></script>
</head>
```

3. We need to add some more markup in the <body> tag. So, go ahead and add the following lines in the <head> section:

```
<div id="main-container">
  <iframe width="560" height="315" frameborder="0" src="http://
www.youtube.com/embed/XSGBVzeBUbk" allowfullscreen> </iframe>
</div>
<script>
  $(document).ready(function(){
    $("#main-container").fitVids();
  });
</script>
```

4. If we preview the results in a browser and begin to resize the browser window, the video will resize automatically:

We're not forced to have to use FitVids, although it is a popular choice; there are others available that will work in a similar manner, such as the following:

- FluidVids, from `http://toddmotto.com/fluid-and-responsive-youtube-and-vimeo-videos-with-fluidvids-js/`

- SimpleVid, available at `http://johnpolacek.github.io/SimpleVid/`

- ResponsiveVideo, available at `http://cbavota.bitbucket.org/responsive-video/`

As an alternative, and ideal if you're only working with a small number of videos on your site, you can use the online service at `EmbedResponsively.com` to manually make your embedded videos responsive. This works by adding a container in HTML and then styling this to allow its resizing responsively, much in the same way as we do when using the FitVids library.

By now, we've produced video content using the `<video>` tags and seen how we can implement it responsively in our site. We do need to bear in mind the need to make content available on the mobile platform though, so let's take a look at how we can do this now.

Catering to different platforms

It goes without saying that part of responsive design is the need to produce content that will work on mobile devices; otherwise it wouldn't be responsive! We could spend lots of time trying to develop something from the ground up, but there is little point in doing so. Others have already produced players that work on a desktop.

With a little extra effort, we can make the players responsive. Thankfully, Neil Gee of the Coolest Guides on the Planet site has already done the hard work for us. Let's take a look at one example player to see how he has made it responsive; we'll use VideoJS for the purposes of our demo. Perform the following steps for this demo:

1. We'll start by extracting the `player` folder from the code download that accompanies this book and save it to our project folder. It contains a working example of the video player, already configured for use. We'll add the necessary changes to make it responsive.

2. In `player.html`, modify the links to the CSS style sheets, shown as follows:

```
<link rel="stylesheet" href="css/video-js.css">
<link rel="stylesheet" href="css/video-js-
  overrides.css">
<script src="js/video.js"></script>
```

3. Next, in a new file, add the following CSS style rules and save it as `video-js-overrides.css`:

```
.video-js { padding-top: 56.25% }
.vjs-fullscreen { padding-top: 0px }
.vjs-default-skin .vjs-big-play-button { left: 40%; top:
  45%; width: 10%; }

// These two media queries resize and reposition the big
  play button to the center of the screen
@media only screen and (max-width:599px) {
  .vjs-default-skin .vjs-big-play-button {top: 45%; width:
    25%;}
}

@media only screen and (min-width:600px) and (max-
  width:768px) {
  .vjs-default-skin .vjs-big-play-button { top: 40%;
  width: 25%;font-size:5em; }
    }
```

4. If we preview the results in a browser, we will see the video play normally. For better results, it is recommended to use Google Chrome. We can emulate different devices using the Developer Toolbar, as indicated in the following screenshot:

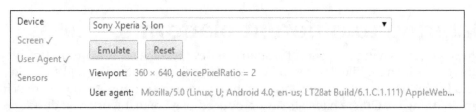

5. Selecting the **Sony Xperia S, Ion** option produces the following result in Chrome. In the following screenshot, the screen has been flipped into landscape mode by changing the **Resolution** options in the **Screen** tab of Developer Toolbar:

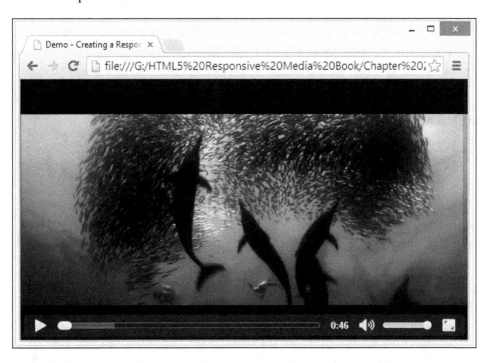

Try changing the options to emulate different devices; you will begin to see that no matter what size is set, the player is still able to play properly.

There is a completed example available in the code download, as player-finished.html and player-finished.css. Rename both files to player.html and player.css to see the finished article. Other video players have had similar treatment by Neil—you can see articles for them at http://coolestguidesontheplanet.com/videodrome/videojs/.

Allowing for vendor prefixes

While working on our code, have you noticed anything in particular, such as the apparent lack of need for vendor prefixes? That's right, to produce a basic responsive solution for a video doesn't require any, so it would be right to ask why we're now talking about needing to allow for them in our code!

The answer lies not in providing the basic styling needed to handle the `<video>` or `<iframe>` tags, but when we move into the realms of setting our video to display full screen or in the background. The former still needs vendor prefixes. While we could provide them manually, it is considered better practice to automatically add them at compilation.

 Before we go any further, this demo requires Node to be installed; this is available at `http://nodejs.org/`. Go ahead and install it for your platform before continuing.

Let's look at using the Autoprefixer plugin for Grunt, which ties in with the service from `http://www.caniuse.com`; the Grunt plugin is available at `https://github.com/postcss/autoprefixer`. The following steps will help you understand the process of adding prefixes:

1. We'll start by creating a new folder for our compilation. In our example, I will use `g:\grunt`; if you use something else, then adjust accordingly.

2. Within the folder, add a new folder called `build` and add three new files under it, namely `gruntfile.js`, `package,json`, and `style.css`, as shown in the following screenshot:

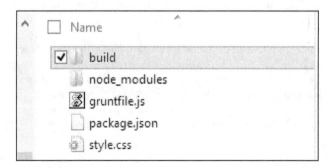

3. In the `gruntfile.js` file, add the following code:

```
module.exports = function (grunt) {
  grunt.initConfig({
    autoprefixer: {
      dist: {
        files: {'build/style.css': 'style.css'}
      }
    },
    watch: {
      styles: {
        files: ['style.css'],
        tasks: ['autoprefixer']
      }
    }
  });
  grunt.loadNpmTasks('grunt-autoprefixer');
  grunt.loadNpmTasks('grunt-contrib-watch');
};
```

4. In `package.json`, add the following code:

```
{
  "name":"yourprojectname",
  "version":"0.0.1",
  "devDependencies":{
    "grunt":"*",
    "grunt-contrib-watch":"*",
    "grunt-autoprefixer":"*"
  }
}
```

5. From the Node command prompt, enter and run the following command to install Autoprefixer and a watch facility:

```
npm install grunt-cli grunt-contrib-watch grunt-autoprefixer
```

6. Node will run through installing all of the dependencies automatically. When completed, we can then run the following line at the prompt to start Grunt watching for any changes:

```
Grunt watch
```

7. We can then make a change to the `style.css` file, such as adding the following line of code:

```
a { width: calc(50% - 2em); transition: width 2s; }
```

We will see Grunt kick in and recompile our code automatically:

```
G:\grunt>grunt watch
Running "watch" task
Waiting...
>> File "style.css" changed.
Running "autoprefixer:dist" (autoprefixer) task
File build/style.css created.

Done, without errors.
Completed in 2.623s at Sun Aug 24 2014 17:36:02 GMT+0100 (GMT Summer Time) - Wai
ting...
```

We can verify that Autoprefixer has done its magic by looking at the `style.css` file that will have appeared in the build folder. While our example was a little simplistic, the functionality will become very useful in our next demo, which uses a number of CSS3 vendor-prefixed properties and where Autoprefixer could cater to this as part of the compilation process.

 If you prefer to use a non-command line alternative, then Autoprefixer for SublimeText is worth a look; it's available at `http://www.hongkiat.com/blog/css-automatic-vendor-prefix/`.

Let's move on and take a look something different. How often have you come across sites that play videos full size when launched? It's a really cool effect, although it must be done with care. Let's take a look at how we can implement this in practice.

Displaying full-size videos

So far, we've covered a lot of theory about creating responsive videos. Now it's time to have a little fun! If we look on the Internet, we will see plenty of examples where designers have created sites that display videos full-size in the background when viewing content.

There are plenty of examples online of how to achieve this. We're going to use the jQuery Cover plugin created by Swedish developer Anton Trollbäck, which is available for download from `https://github.com/antontrollback/cover`. Let's make our video appear in its full size using the following steps:

1. Firstly, from the code download that accompanies this book, extract a copy of `fullsize.html`. It contains some basic markup, which uses the HTML5 video tags to include two videos in MP4 and WebM format along with some text in an overlay.

2. In `fullsize.html`, add the following lines immediately below the `<title>` statement:

```
<link rel="stylesheet" href="css/fullsize.css">
<script src="js/jquery.min.js"></script>
<script src="js/jquery.cover.js"></script>
<script>
  $(document).ready(function() {
    $('video').cover({
      ratio: 1080 / 1920
    });

    $(window).resize(function() {
      $('video').cover('set');
    });
  });
</script>
```

3. Next, add the following lines to the foot of the `fullsize.css` file and save it to the `css` subfolder in your project folder:

```
#overlay { border: 1px solid #000; padding: 10px; width:
  30%;
opacity: 0.8; background-color: #000; margin-left: auto;
  margin-right: auto; color: #fff; font-weight: bold; font-
  family: arial, helvetica; border-radius: 4px; margin-top:
  5%; }
video { margin-top: -5%; }
```

4. From the code download, copy across the `bigbuckbunny.mp4` and `bigbuckbunny.webm` videos and store these in the `video` subfolder within your project folder. We will also need the `jquery.js` and `jquery.cover.js` files as well, so copy these into the `js` subfolder.

At this stage, we should have a working demo. So go ahead and preview the results in a browser; if all is well, you should see the video play without sound, as shown in the following screenshot:

Now we can simply play the video in full view when it's opened.

 There is a working example within the code bundle for this demo. Rename the `fullsize-finished.html` file to `fullsize.html` and the `fullsize-finished.css` file to `fullsize.css` before viewing the finished article.

Creating full size videos produces an intriguing effect, which needs to be managed with care. There are a few points to consider:

- Use Modernizr (or similar tool) to detect if a mobile device is in use. If so, then display a background image instead.
- This feature is useful for big announcements, where content needs to be displayed for a finite period of time—it will lose its appeal quickly though!
- Don't set the video to display sound; this will only put people off from visiting your site.
- If you use a poster image, try to keep the file size to a minimum, without reducing the quality too much.

- Try to provide some mechanism whereby the video can be turned off if needed. Not everyone will want to see it running.

- You may want to consider using something like the Network API to gauge the user's Internet connection. If they don't have a fast connection, then a smaller video should be played instead or the facility will be bypassed entirely for that user.

Ultimately, it is worth giving this some careful consideration before implementing such a facility. If done well, it can produce a superb effect; there is a fine line that is all too easily crossed! This kind of effect would work well on music artists' websites. For some intriguing examples, take a look at `http://www.creative bloq.com/web-design/video-backgrounds-2131982`. Hopefully, this will give you some inspiration for your next project!

Summary

We've come to the end of our journey through responsive video, where we've covered a variety of useful effects. Let's take a moment to consider what we've covered in this chapter. We began with a brief look at video formats that work well with responsive video design; as part of this, we covered how easy it is to convert other formats into one of the recognized HTML5 video formats.

We then looked at embedding content into a page, using standard HTML5 tags, and noted some of the issues that appear. We then moved on and took a look at determining how we can get the available viewport size, as a replacement for media queries when working with videos. We then took a look at catering to support for other formats, followed by a look at using JavaScript libraries to provide fall back support for videos.

We then covered how you can provide support for different mobile platforms, using popular video players such as VideoJS. We then finished with a look at providing support for full size videos in a website, using the Big Buck Bunny videos created by the Blender Foundation.

So far throughout this book, we've worked with either images or videos. It is unlikely that your site will just require one or the other. In the next chapter, we'll see how to include both and look at the pitfalls of doing so in order to avoid heavy pages and long download times.

3
Mixing Content

Load Times For 69% Of Responsive Design Mobile Sites Deemed "Unacceptable"…

A staggering fact, but absolutely true: a survey carried out by the mobile developer company Tribilis in April 2014 found that for 155 sites surveyed, only 21 percent loaded in four seconds or less on smartphones. Moreover, those that took longer had an average page weight of 1.7 MB.

Sobering thoughts, but ones that perfectly illustrate the pitfalls of mixing videos and images on pages in responsive design! We need to strike a balance between displaying the right media content that is not too large or too small while keeping our page load times small. This chapter works through some examples and details some of the pitfalls associated with mixing content, which can lead to heavy pages and long download times.

We'll cover a number of topics in this chapter, which will include:

- Mixing video and image content on the same page
- Considering limitations of mixing content
- Using preloaders to reduce delays
- Adding lazy loading support to our pages
- Making allowances for mobile devices

Intrigued? Let's make a start!

Mixing video and image content on the same page

Throughout this book, we've seen some of the tips and tricks we need to use to make our media content responsive and worked through some examples of the styles we need to implement to make this happen.

However, it is unlikely that every responsive site will have either images or videos; it is more likely that there will be a mix of both on at least some sites! This can present its own issues, so to see what can happen, let's run through a simple demo.

From the code download, extract the `code` folder for this chapter and save it to your project folder; this contains a simple demo that shows the issues we face with mixing videos and images together in a responsive design. If we run the `mix-responsive.html` demo as it stands, it would appear to look okay from the start until we scroll down and view the video. The layout is not ideal, but there are a few changes we can make:

- The banner image at the top of the browser window is too large. While this may be okay on a desktop, it will choke smartphones; it needs to be resized.
- The embedded video isn't respecting the boundaries of its container, with the result that it is spilling out over the whole page, making the text difficult to view.
- We can improve on the use of the banner. Once we've changed it to a thinner design, we can then add a media query to switch in a smaller version of this thinner design.

Fortunately, these are easy fixes to make. Let's see what is involved:

1. Save a copy of `mix-responsive.html` and `mix-responsive.css` as `mix-responsiveV2.html` and `mix-responsiveV2.css` respectively (in the same folder). Don't forget to change the link to the CSS file from within our HTML markup to point to the new file!

2. Look for the `banner` div on or around line 28 and remove the `<img>` tags, so the HTML markup is as shown in the following line of code:

   ```
   <div id="banner"></div>
   ```

3. Further down, look for `<video controls>` on or around line 34; we need to encompass it within a wrapper `<div>`:

   ```
   <div id="video-wrapper">
     <video controls>
       <source src="video/bigbuckbunny-480px.mp4" type="video/mp4">
       <source src="video/bigbuckbunny-480px.webm" type="video/webm">
     </video>
   </div>
   ```

4. Open up `mix-responsiveV2.css` and add the following styles:

```
#video-wrapper video { max-width: 100%; }
#banner { background-image: url('../img/abstract-banner-
  large.jpg'); height: 15.31rem; width: 45.5rem; max-width:
  100%; }

@media screen and (max-width: 30rem) {
  #banner { margin-top: 150px; background-image:
    url('../img/abstract-banner-medium.jpg'); height:
    4.85rem; width: 45.5rem; max-width: 100%; }
}
```

5. Save the files. If we preview the results of our work in a browser, we can see a significant improvement in the appearance of our page.

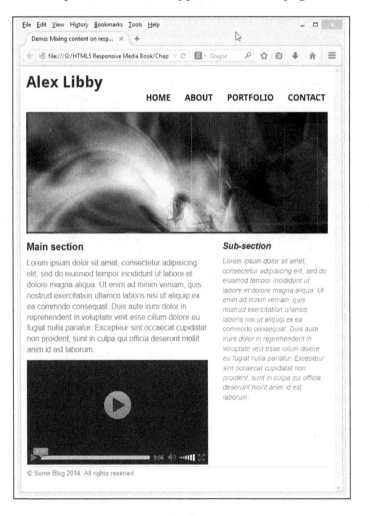

Try resizing the page now; you should see that the video and image elements will resize perfectly, without any spillage. In a nutshell, our changes have been very simple. We've added a container to the video to which we've added the `max-width` style attribute and set this to `100%`. We then switched out the bulky banner to a thinner version, setting this to retain the full width of its container when resized. It is switched to a smaller version once we go below a screen width of `30rem`.

There is a completed version of our demo with the fixes in place. In the code download, look for and extract `mix-responsiveV2-finished.html` and `mix-responsiveV2-finished.css`. Save both to the same places as the original files to view the results.

Before we move on and take a look at how we can make allowances for mobile devices when mixing content, I want to cover off a couple of tips that might help give you a little inspiration:

- We've embedded the video directly in the page. It works perfectly well, but if we wanted to give it a little extra sparkle, we could consider using an overlay. There are plenty available, but one good (responsive) example is FrescoJS, available at `http://www.frescojs.com/`.

- There may be a need to resort to jQuery to provide the responsive functionality for an element if CSS3 is not supported. Older browsers such as IE8 or below might fall into this category. We can do this using something such as Embedly jQuery, available at `http://embedly.github.io/embedly-jquery/`.

There is a tutorial available on how to configure Embedly jQuery at `http://embed.ly/docs/tutorials/responsive`.

- If you need to add responsive code for third-party embedded videos (such as YouTube), you can use the service at `http://embedresponsively.com/`; simply enter the URL of any video or image to embed and click on **Embed** to get the code.

Okay! On we go! We've talked a lot about mixing content, but as we've seen from the demo, there are some aspects where there is room for improvement. The alterations we've made in our demo are just some of the pointers we can use to remove some of the pitfalls of mixing content, so let's take a look at a few in more detail.

Considering the pitfalls of mixing content

Responsive design has become hugely popular over the last few years, with visitors browsing content on the Internet using a variety of devices. This increases the pressure on developers to ensure that their sites work well on a range of different devices and platforms. A recent study by eMarketeer illustrates that four out of every five people will access content via a mobile device and that this figure is projected to increase over the next three years.

Region	2014	2015	2016	2017
Middle East and Africa	94.0	94.0	95.0	96.0
Asia Pacific	87.4	90.0	92.6	93.9
Central and Eastern Europe	72.4	80.6	86.6	91.7
North America	64.3	69.8	74.4	79.2
Western Europe	67.8	78.2	85.0	90.6
Latin America	58.5	65.0	70.1	75.2
Worldwide	**79.1**	**83.6**	**87.3**	**90.1**

The figures in the preceding table are percentage values taken from eMarketeer in December 2013.

So that we don't fall into the trap of producing a responsive site that offers a poor experience, let's take a look at some of the pitfalls we need to consider when mixing media sources in responsive design:

- The size and number of images on a page will directly affect how quickly your visitors can view the page. To reduce the impact, we can use several techniques:
  - Image compression is the first simple technique widely used. For a perfect example of the need to compress images, an article by Tribilis makes for interesting reading, available at `http://blog.trilibis.com/trilibis-web-performance-survey-finds-69-percent-of-responsive-design-websites-fail-to-deliver-acceptable-load-times-on-mobile-devices-02759`. It shows some significant gains when images are compressed!
  - The next important technique is the conversion of small images into data URIs or as part of an image sprite.
  - Another technique is the use of lazy loading to only show those images that are visible within the viewport.

- We need to be aware of the breakpoints in our design and alter our media queries to suit. What may have worked well for images may not work equally as well for videos, particularly if they are of different sizes.

- Scaling smaller images to a larger size will result in the loss of quality; it is recommended to start with large size images and dynamically resize them for smaller devices. Once we get to a particular breakpoint, then we can switch to using a smaller image by default to avoid images becoming illegible if they have not been sized for a particular breakpoint / viewport width.

- Scaling images can cause issues when they are reduced to a very small size. The dimensions are likely to mean that we can't view the image properly, its meaning will be lost, the file size won't be any smaller, and it may be better to simply not display it instead.

- Consider converting vector images to the SVG format. Conversion to standard image formats such as JPG, GIF, or PNG will likely lead to the same loss of quality as scaling small images to a larger size. SVG images scale well without any loss of quality.

- If your site uses video, then one pitfall that can trip you up is the format used. Although we only need to encode for MP4 or WebM support, not every device will use both. A careful analysis of web metrics should help us understand which operating systems are used to access the site and therefore help determine which format of video to use.

 For an up-to-date check on format support, take a look at the articles available at http://www.jwplayer.com/html5.

- Do you use images for small elements such as buttons? If so, consider converting them to CSS3 equivalents, at least for the browsers that can support them. It will mean a reduction in requests to the server (we're not calling the images) and the CSS style sheet would have been cached by the browser, so the response will be quicker. There are plenty of examples available online; you can try Chris Coyier's Button creator at http://css-tricks.com/examples/ButtonMaker/ or CSS Shape Generator at http://html-generator.weebly.com/css-shape-generator.html.

- Specifying only the width of images may cause a doubling or tripling of the cycles that many browsers must process to layout the new resized page. While each of these cycles typically take less than a millisecond, they stack up, especially if there are multiple scalable elements on the page. Addressing the height in the same declaration can reduce this issue:

```
img, video { max-width: 100%; height: auto; }
```

- If your site needs to display videos in 4:3 or 16:9 ratio format, then these may not resize properly. We can get around this using a wrapper in HTML that is styled to the proper dimensions, then stretch the video to fit the following container:

```
<div class="wrapper-with-intrinsic-ratio">
   <div class="element-to-stretch"></div>
</div>
```

The CSS styling would look something like this:

```
.wrapper-with-intrinsic-ration {
  position: relative; height: 0;
  padding-top: 25px; /* to allow for the player chrome */
  padding-bottom: 56.25%  /* 9:16 = 0.5625 */
}

.element-to-stretch { position: absolute; top: 0; left: 0;
  width: 100%; height: 100%; background: teal; }
```

Phew! There are certainly plenty of places where we can be tripped up if we're not careful! Let's move on and take a look at a couple of tricks we can use to help manage media content in our pages, beginning with a look at preloading images.

Using preloaders to reduce delays

Preloading content is not a new concept in the world of web design. The idea is to reduce the amount of time it takes to view the page in a browser, as some (or all) of the content has been fetched ahead of viewing the page and cached in the browser.

There are plenty of examples available using JavaScript (such as PreloadJS at http://www.createjs.com/#!/PreloadJS). But this adds an extra overhead to our pages that we can avoid, particularly in a responsive design.

Instead, we can use CSS to achieve the same effect, provided the styles and images are called at the right time. This way, they will be ready for us when we render the images on screen.

 For the purposes of this demo, I've simplified the code to concentrate on the preloading process only.

Let's take a look at preloading in action with a simple demo:

1. From the code download that accompanies this book, extract a copy of `preloading.html` and then save it in our project folder.

2. Next, extract `img01.png` to `img04.png` from the code download. The images should go into a subfolder marked `img` in our project folder.

3. In a new file, add the following styles to a new CSS style sheet. Save this as `preloading.css`, in a `css` subfolder within our project folder:

```
html { font-family: Verdana, Arial, Helvetica, sans-serif;
   }
body { margin: 60px auto 0; padding: 0; background-color:
   #606061; color: #ffffff; }
img { border: none; padding: 10px; max-width: 100%;}
p { font-size: 1em; margin: 0 0 1em 0; }
#container { position: absolute; top: 0; left: 0;
   background-color: #18191d; width: 100%; height: 40px; }
#container p { color: #ffffff; margin: 10px auto 0; text-
   align: center; width: 310px; }
#preload { margin-left: auto; margin-right: auto; width:
   900px; }


body:before {
   content: url(../img/img01.png) no-repeat -9999px -9999px,
            url(../img/img02.png) no-repeat -9999px -
               9999px,
      url(../img/img03.png) no-repeat -9999px -9999px,
      url(../img/img04.png) no-repeat -9999px -9999px;
   display: none;
}
```

Before we preview our work, it's useful to take a quick look to see how this process works. The key to it is the class added to the body to retrieve the images before we use them later in our code:

```
<body class="preload-images">
  <div id="container">
...
  <div id="preload">
    <img src="img/img01.png" alt="Image 01" />
...
```

If we preview the results of our work, we'll see the following four images appear:

The beauty about using this method is that we've removed the need to have to use yet another library, such as PreloadJS. Instead, we can now choose to call it if we decide to provide support for older browsers that don't support the `body:before` trick we used in our demo.

Let's change tack and look at the reverse side of this coin—lazy loading. No, this is not some form of getting up on a Sunday morning after a particularly good night out (terrible joke!), but a means to only load and display images at the point of viewing them. Intrigued? I will reveal all as part of our next exercise.

Adding lazy loading support to our pages

One of the primary aims of responsive design should be the consideration of any tactic we can use to reduce the overall loading time of our pages; this is particularly true for mobile devices.

So far, you've seen how we can preload content. In some instances, this may not be ideal; instead, we can do the opposite and not load content until we are about to view it:

This process is known as lazy loading; it effectively removes the focus of loading the images from the front (that is, on loading of the page) to the point of when we need to see the images. To illustrate the process, we're going to use the bLazy plugin by Bjørn Klinggard, available at http://dinbror.dk/blog/blazy/. The great thing about this library is that it is lightweight and written in pure JavaScript, so has a zero dependency count! Oh and did I forget— it's responsive too.

Let's take a quick look at a demo (based on the original by the author), which we could easily use as a basis for something more involved within any responsive design:

1. For the purposes of this demo, extract a copy of the lazy loading folder within the code download that accompanies this book. It contains the markup files, images, styling, and JavaScript needed for our demo.

2. Run the lazyloading.html file. Notice how only the first few images show? If we scroll down, we can see the green loading image appear with the next image appearing after a short delay.

The magic in this demo centers on this code excerpt from the demo:

```
<div class="wrapper ratio_big-img loading">
    <img class="b-lazy" src=img/placeholder.png data-
        src="img/big-bear7.jpg" data-src-small="img/small-
        bear7.jpg" alt="Lazy load images image7" />
</div>
```

We kick off with a placeholder image. In this instance, we're using a 1 px square PNG file that could be easily converted to its data-URI equivalent with little overhead. We then use two `data-src` tags to flip between either the small or large versions of the image when the window is resized.

We can test to ensure that the pictures are indeed only being loaded when visible. In this instance, using Firefox's **Developer** toolbar, we can see each URL loaded when viewed in the **Console** tab, as indicated in the following screenshot:

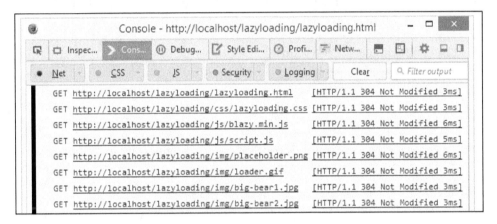

 A small point to remember — in this instance, the preceding screenshot shows the use of a local webserver; the principle works the same whether the images are loaded from the filesystem or through a web server.

This demo is perfect as a basis to display a gallery effect on a site, particularly when viewed on a mobile device. With a bit of reconfiguration, we could even set it to display retina-based images; although that is something I will leave for you as a challenge! Let's move on and cover a key topic when designing responsively: the need to make allowances for mobile devices.

Making allowances for mobile devices

Adding visual content to our pages will begin to bring the site alive, but we should bear in mind the increase in latency times. Latency is a major killer on mobile devices; if we take a 1 MB page with 80 plus requests, for example, loading the page can take over 4 seconds!

Using JavaScript is expensive in terms of resources. It takes time and can block the rendering of pages. A much better alternative is to only load the resource when it is needed. On desktops, this is less of an issue, but becomes crucial for mobile devices. Take, for example, Google's Gmail service—using this principle reduces the latency for loading JavaScript from 2600 ms to just 240 ms. With this in mind, let's take a look at some useful tips we can consider to help reduce the impact of mixing responsive images and videos on a mobile device:

- If we are designing for mobile devices, it is essential to work out which platform our users are using. This will dictate what content can be displayed. One way is that we can use lazy loading (in the form of media queries) to only show images when required:

```
// equivalent to 720px
@media all and (min-width: 45rem) {
  body:after { content: 'desktop'; display: none; }
}
```

Another method encourages conditional loading to only load those elements and styling that are necessary:

```
var size = window.getComputedStyle(document.body,
  ':after').getPropertyValue('content');
if (size == 'desktop') {
// load content here...
}
```

 These methods do not require any additional libraries to be imported. This is ideal if our site is already code-heavy and we want to avoid adding more to our site. In reality though, we may look to use something like RequireJS to manage the importing of files when needed; this does come with the overhead of the RequireJS library though!

- A good practice is to carefully consider whether all of the elements on the page are really needed for a useable mobile experience. Check those social media buttons. For example, some may be larger than you think and while they could be replaced with smaller/lighter versions, it may make better sense to not include them at all for mobile devices. Alternatively, consider loading the larger ones using conditional loading, while smaller ones can be loaded automatically. A great example of an easy replacement is to consider using the FontAwesome icons instead of images. This will help reduce the number of files that need to be loaded by the server (see the next point).

- Consider using data URIs (via a generator service, such as `http://datauri.net/`) or sprites / web fonts (such as Entype or FontAwesome) in place of images. Although data URIs or sprites may not make the code smaller, they will reduce the number of requests to the server. Using web fonts can have the same effect too; we can take it even further with building a custom font using the Fontello service at `http://www.fontello.com`).

- If you are using videos on your site, consider hosting them on YouTube. This will save space and bandwidth costs to your site. In addition, there will be a consistent format, which reduces the risk of any issues where videos can't play on mobile devices.

- Be careful about where you use large, high quality images—on mobile devices, your visitors will not thank you when their data usage goes through the roof! There are plenty of options available to reduce the image size. We will look at two such examples later in this chapter that use Node JS to resize and compress images automatically.

> Alternatively, if you need to display images on high pixel density displays, doubling the size but increasing the compression will help reduce the file size. To see the effect in action, take a look at the tutorial available at `http://greatfridays.com/blog/images-in-responsive-web-development/`. Can you see any difference in quality between the two images used in the PayPal demo?

- Always set videos to show a poster image and not to automatically play for mobile devices. There are many options to produce images (including those that can be automated), so there is no excuse. We'll see one example later in this chapter, which can be easily adapted to produce an extra image to serve as the poster.

- A useful tool to get to grips with is the Page Visibility or Network APIs. This appears very simple to implement, but opens up a variety of possible uses. One such use is to shut off any videos that are playing temporarily if a browser window is not being displayed; this will help reduce bandwidth costs.

- If your site requires a lot of vector images, you will get better results using SVG-formatted files. These are effectively XML files that can resize with no loss of quality.

Enough theory — let's actually try out two of these tips; we could complete them manually, but instead we can take advantage of a task runner to complete them automatically. Intrigued? I will explain all, beginning with a look at creating responsive versions of our chosen images.

Creating responsive images automatically

A key part of providing content for any website is of course images. This becomes all the more important on responsive sites where we've seen that multiple versions of the same image are needed to provide a fluid solution to our responsive needs.

We could of course create each version of the image manually, but this is the 21st century: who wants (or even has the time) to create different sizes manually? Surely there has to be a better way. You'd be right: we can automate the whole process. Let's take a look how using the Node JS task runner as the basis to automate the process.

 This exercise is designed to run as standalone; the principles can easily be applied to a larger, more complex grunt process as you get more accustomed to using Grunt.

Let's make a start by installing Node JS:

1. We'll begin by browsing to `http://nodejs.org/download/` to download the latest version for your platform. It's available for Windows, Mac, and Linux platforms. Double-click on the **MSI installer** and run through the wizard, accepting all defaults.

2. From the code download, extract the `responseimg` folder and save it on your PC.

3. Bring up a Node JS command prompt, then change to the `responseimg` folder and run this command to install `grunt-responsive-images`:

   ```
   npm install
   ```

4. This will install `grunt-responsive-images`, along with the dependencies and Grunt; in this instance, we're using the `grunt-simple-watch` applet to automatically monitor our folder for any changes.

5. At the command prompt, change to the `src` folder and then run the following command:

   grunt autoresize

6. This kicks off the `grunt-simple-watch` plugin to begin automatically monitoring for changes in the `src` folder. In this example, I've already dropped a single JPEG image into the `src` folder, which is also shown in the following screenshot:

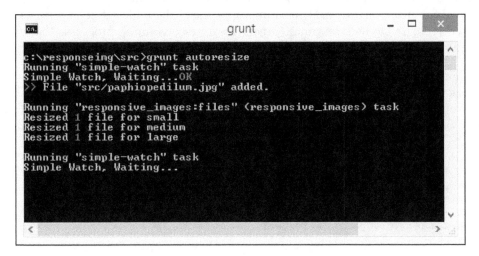

7. Any image dropped into the `src` folder will be used to create three new images, such as the example shown in the following screenshot:

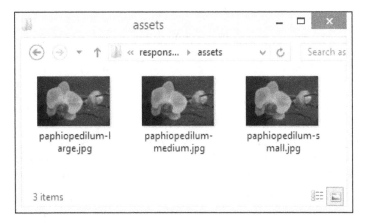

The automated process is now ready for use. We can drop any number of JPEG images into the folder; three new images will be produced for each new image dropped into the folder.

 We're using the default sizes for each image as specified in the plugin; these can be easily customized in the options for the plugin within our gruntfile.js file.

Automating the shrinking process

We can of course develop this automation further. It's definitely worth reading up on the capabilities of Node and checking out some of the wide range of plugins that have been created to help automate otherwise time-consuming processes that do not add any value when done manually.

Let's take a look at one way of extending our automated process. We've set up a process to create the images, but there is a likelihood that some of the images are not compressed as much as they could be. We can fix that by adding in support for compression, using the grunt-contrib-imagemin plugin:

1. Open up a copy of the gruntfile.js file. We first need to add in support for the grunt-contrib-imagemin plugin, so go ahead and modify the line as shown in the following code snippet:

   ```
   files: ['src/*.jpg'],
   tasks: ['responsive_images', 'imagemin'],
   options: {
   ```

2. Next, alter the code to add in the block for imagemin task as shown in the following code snippet:

   ```
       dest: '../responseimg/assets'
         }
       },
       imagemin: {
         jpg: { options: { progressive: false }, files: [{ expand:
   true, cwd: 'assets/', src: '*.jpg', dest: 'assets/', ext: '.jpg'
   }]
       }
   ```

3. When running the task in Grunt, we need to tell it to load in the grunt-contrib-imagemin plugin, so go ahead and add this line into the gruntfile.js file as indicated in the following lines of code:

   ```
   grunt.loadNpmTasks('grunt-responsive-images');
   grunt.loadNpmTasks('grunt-contrib-imagemin');
   ```

4. We need to make one final change, so go ahead and alter the following line as shown:

```
grunt.registerTask('default', ['simple-watch']);
```

5. Bring up a NodeJS command prompt and run the following command to add the plugin and its dependencies to the package.json file:

```
npm install grunt-contrib-imagemin --save-dev
```

6. We're now ready to test our Grunt package. In the command prompt, change the directory to the project folder, then run this command:

```
grunt
```

7. If all is well, we'll see the Grunt task run and successfully produce three new images, which are then compressed.

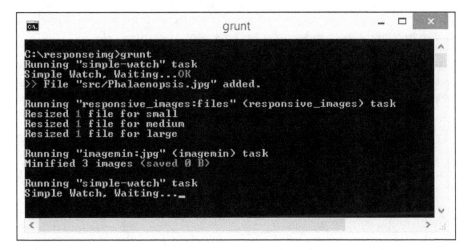

The automation process is now ready for use. Although we've only put one image through the process, we could at this point put many images through. I would recommend running some tests to gauge how many you can safely process at the same time, as this will be dependent on resources in your PC or Mac.

Summary

Phew! We've certainly packed a lot into a small space! Let's recap on what you've learned throughout this chapter. We kicked off with a demo of mixing video and image content, initially to see firsthand some of the issues we face when mixing content, but then to use some of the tips and tricks you've learned to get the pages to behave responsively.

Having looked at a demo, we then moved onto considering some of the pitfalls of mixing content; we saw how the large increase in responsive use has increased over the last few years making it crucial that our designs work on a variety of platforms. We covered a number of tips we can use to make allowances for mobile platforms in our designs.

We ended the chapter looking at two demos using NodeJS to automate the creation of different versions of our images and automatically shrinking them; this illustrates how we can automate the process and save us a lot of manual effort.

Now that we have our content, we need to test it thoroughly to ensure it works across a wide range of devices. We'll take a look at the testing process in the next chapter, examining some of the considerations and pitfalls we need to be aware of when working with responsive media.

4
Testing Responsive Media

Yikes! What do I test? iPads? iPhones? Which Android devices? Such questions must have definitely crossed your mind. Worry not! This chapter will guide you through some really cool testing techniques/methods.

Testing is a key part of the process of working with responsive media. We need to test our content thoroughly on a variety of different browsers, devices, and platforms to ensure we don't encounter any problems when our site is released to the wild.

It is possible you might think we need lots of specialist technology—nothing could be further from the truth! Throughout this chapter, we'll see how easy it is to test sites with nothing more than different browsers or online emulators. We'll take a look at some of the considerations and pitfalls we need to be mindful of and see how we can easily make improvements to those sites that aren't running as well as they should. We'll cover the following topics:

- Considering the pitfalls of testing responsive media
- Testing responsive sites using emulators
- Using tools to determine speed
- Working through a theoretical example of slowness

Ready? Let's get started!

A starting point for testing

You've created that killer app or website and are ready to release it to the wild... or are you?

Before we release our creations into the wild, we need to test them thoroughly. It goes without saying that each and every element needs to be tested, but media such as images or videos need particular attention.

If the thought of testing conjures up images of needing lots of automated scripts, rigorous checking, and specialist software, think again. The most useful tool is the one we already have—our browser!

Granted, we need to perform lots of tests to ensure our content works well in a range of different devices. However, most of our testing can be done in desktop browsers, which come with responsive design facilities built within. They are not perfect, so we need the assistance of other facilities to complement our testing. Let's make a start though and take a look at the responsive facilities on offer in each browser, beginning with Chrome.

 It should be noted that commands given will be for Windows; for Mac users, we have *Cmd* + *Opt* in place of *Ctrl* + *Shift*.

Using Google Chrome or Opera

For testing responsive sites, Google Chrome is a hard act to beat. It offers the widest range of options to help with proving how well a responsive site works.

We can use it to change the user agent, alter the screen resolution, and even test retina-enabled devices; to enable the responsive design mode in Chrome is as simple as pressing *Ctrl* + *Shift* + *I*:

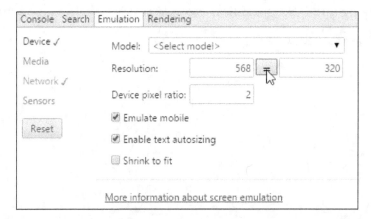

Opera's browser is almost identical. The responsive emulator can be enabled in the same manner, although some of the options are in slightly different locations.

Using Firefox

Not to be outdone, Firefox boasts a responsive design mode too; it is more simplistic than Chrome, but nonetheless serves a useful purpose. Firefox's **Responsive Design View** can be enabled by pressing *Ctrl + Shift + M*:

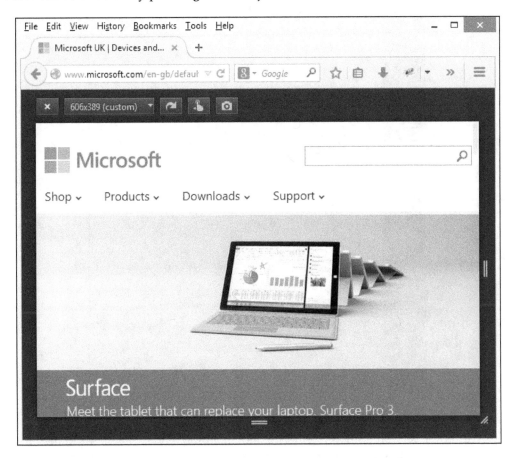

 Try clicking on the **606 x 389 (custom)** drop-down item and selecting a new value. Firefox will automatically resize the viewport to the new size; if the new screen size is larger, you will need to resize the browser window.

Using Internet Explorer

Internet Explorer takes a different approach to responsive design. To get the best emulation options requires the use of the latest version of the browser, which is version 11 at the time of this writing. The responsive emulation settings are held within the **Developer** toolbar (press *F12* to enable this), then switch to the **Emulation** tab to alter the settings:

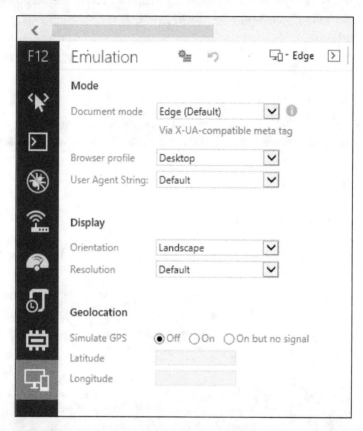

The key to testing using the desktop browser is twofold – they will give a reasonable approximation of what your site will look like in a mobile view and should act only as a starting point to your testing. The real tests will come when we start to use online testing services. These offer the opportunity to test over a number of devices at once, although there is no substitution for the real thing! We'll cover use of these services later in this chapter, in the *Testing responsive sites with online tools* section.

Some alternatives to consider

While most testing is best completed online, there are a couple of options you may like to consider: Google Chrome has a more comprehensive browser add-in that emulates many online testing services. It's available at `http://www.dimensionstoolkit.com/`. Adobe has released Adobe Edge Inspect, which attempts to link your local development site to a mobile emulator. It's available through Apple iTunes—more details are available at `http://html.adobe.com/edge/inspect/`.

So far we've seen that the only way to effectively test your site is manually, in as wide a range of browsers as possible, on different platforms. This is not without pitfalls. Let's take a moment to consider some of the traps that may trip us up, if we're not careful when testing our work.

Considering pitfalls of responsive testing

Who says testing is ever easy? This is true in most projects, but particularly so when testing responsive sites. We've concentrated on working with responsive media throughout this book, but many of the pitfalls we are likely to encounter will equally apply at a site level and not just to images or videos. The following list gives us an idea of such pitfalls:

- Which devices should you test? To some degree, this will depend on researching your target market. But it should be a wide range to include both Android and iOS devices and popular mobile browsers such as Chrome, Opera Mini, and Dolphin.

We clearly can't test for every device, so use of Google Analytics is key to establishing a good range of devices that should be used. A great example of how testing has helped influence a company's responsive design is Marriot hotels. They found that their mobile site uncovered a number of issues with how their homepage was being displayed. Fixing these played an influential part in the design and construction of their responsive site offer.

 You can read the full article about the testing performed by Marriot at http://www.mobilemarketer.com/cms/news/software-technology/18494.html.

- What do your customers want to do on a mobile device? Is creating a seamless site that works for all devices and platforms the right thing to do or should you segment functionality based on what tasks your mobile users are asking for? Being selective about what is on offer on a mobile platform in relation to a full-sized site can act as a gauge of how useful a truly responsive site would be to your users.

- A speed test is crucial. This will determine how well your site works on good or bad Wi-Fi connections, 4G, 3G, and EDGE; all of these should be tested (particularly EDGE, if you can find it!).

- Do you have access to colleagues, friends, or willing participants who can help test your site? Do they have the right devices that fit in with your test plans, so you can ensure you've covered enough devices?

 The reality is that anyone spending time developing responsive content will need to build up a pool of devices. If you work alone, then this may take some time; Brad Frost has put together some useful tips on how to test on real devices without it becoming too expensive. You can read his comments at http://bradfrostweb.com/blog/mobile/test-on-real-mobile-devices-without-breaking-the-bank/.

- There are plenty of emulators online to test responsive sites, but how well do they work? These will give you a feel for how well the site should work, but there is no substitute for testing on a real device!

- Screen resolution will play a major role. Resizing a site on a desktop with 1600 x 900 pixels will look different on a five-inch screen of a Galaxy S4, which will also be different to the 1334 x 750 pixel screen of a 4.7-inch retina display of an Apple iPhone 6. Not only will content appear much smaller, but images will differ when displayed on retina-enabled devices.

- The use of media queries on your site will mean content may not be at the same location on the page, or even be displayed. This leads to an uneven playing field when testing, making automation impossible, and leading to increased costs of manual effort and resource.

- Design strategies and approaches will differ between devices, making it difficult to test consistently across a range of devices. For instance, a hover interaction on a desktop will not transfer to a mobile device; links on one device can act differently on others. It requires the skill of an experienced tester to allow for these differences and to avoid applying tests incorrectly, which would result in inadequate coverage.

The key point when testing is that nothing is ever consistent. Testing for one device or platform is not always likely to be the same for others! This is where the skill of an experienced tester will come into play. Ultimately, the level of testing performed on as wide a range of different devices will determine the success or failure of any responsive site.

Testing responsive sites with online tools

We've already seen that initial testing of our sites is possible in most desktop browsers, but there is a drawback to this approach. These tools will be set to display a limited set of screen sizes, which will require an update of the browser application to reflect any changes.

To help bolster our testing, we can use one of any number of online emulators. This has the advantage of dynamic resizing (by changing the size of the browser window), as well as choosing from any one of a number of preset sizes. While we may not be able to emulate the device perfectly, we can at least ensure that content will render correctly at a desired size.

Take, for example, Microsoft's site—when viewed using the ScreenFly emulator (available at `http://www.quirktools.com/screenfly`)—set to display as a Motorola RAZR V8, it displays perfectly within the 240 x 320 pixel display that would be present on this device:

The site is clearly responsive—the images from the desktop version have been resized and repositioned and the menu system reworked to suit a mobile display. It's worth taking a look at some of the styles that are being set. Remember how we used the basic principle of using percentages, rather than fixed `em` or `rem` (or even `pixel`) values? The same principle is being applied here, where the main image immediately below the menu is resized to `166.5%` of its size.

We can prove this with a quick peek in a DOM inspector such as Firebug:

Notice the styles highlighted in the screenshot? This is a perfect example of what we talked about back in *Chapter 1, Working with Responsive Images*. Simply changing our image sizes to use percentages will go a long way to making a site responsive. Try resizing the browser window and notice how the values change in the DOM inspector.

In contrast, the Packt Publishing website (`www.packtpub.com`) is displayed in the same ScreenFly emulator:

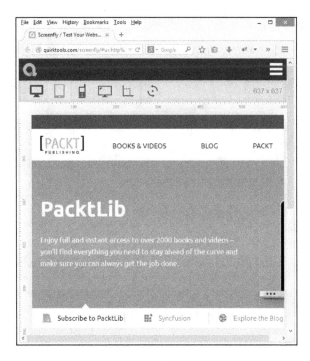

ScreenFly, in this instance, is set to emulate a Kindle Fire at 800 x 600 pixels. The site clearly needs some work. The images are not responsive, with the result that the jumbotron at the top of the page is not fully displayed.

There are dozens of responsive emulators available for use. They all follow very similar principles, although they are likely to be more up to date, in terms of device sizes, than standard desktop browsers. The following are some alternatives to try:

- Mat Kersley's simple responsive tester available at `http://mattkersley.com/responsive/`
- Responsinator available at `http://www.responsinator.com/`
- Media Genesis' Responsive Design Checker available at `http://responsivedesignchecker.com/`
- OpenDeviceLab.com available at `http://opendevicelab.com/`
- Viewport Resizer by Malte Wasserman available at `http://lab.maltewassermann.com/viewport-resizer/`
- BrowserShots available at `http://browsershots.org/`
- BrowserStack available at `http://www.browserstack.com/`

A good site is Am I Responsive available at `http://ami.responsivedesign.is` — this shows the site in a number of common devices at the same time:

Although the content appears very small, we can at least interact with the website to get a feel for how it works, and begin to see where there may be areas for improvement. Ultimately, it doesn't matter though how small or large your site is; if it crawls along at a snail's pace, then it will put visitors off. Fortunately, we can easily see if this is likely to become an issue for any site we operate as a precursor to tweaking elements to improve access.

Using tools to determine speed

There are plenty of ways to determine if our site is running slowly—arguably one of the most well known is YSlow by Yahoo available at `https://developer.yahoo.com/yslow/`. In the following screenshot, it is shown in use from within Firebug:

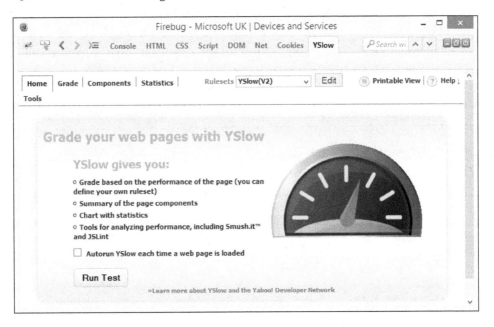

YSlow is perfect to establish where there are slow elements in our pages. It uses a number of rules based on research by Yahoo's Exceptional Performance Team to work out how well a site measures up against its standards for performance.

Let's take a look at using it to see if some well-known sites could be improved. As an example, we'll begin with installing YSlow as a plugin for Firefox.

>
> This example assumes we are using Firefox with Firebug already installed; if it is not already present, then you can download and install it from `http://www.getfirebug.com`.

There are various ways to install YSlow. They include using a bookmarklet, browser add-ins, or working directly from the command line. The most convenient is a browser plugin, so we can assess a site directly:

1. Let's start by browsing to `https://developer.yahoo.com/yslow/` and clicking on **Firefox** under **Availability** to install the Firefox add-on.

2. At this point, follow the instructions — the add-on installs using the normal process for Firefox plugins.

At this point, we are ready to start using YSlow:

1. Browse to `http://www.microsoft.com` and resize the window to a smaller size; the aim is to emulate the appearance of working on a smaller device.

2. Click on the Firebug icon or go to **View | Firebug**, then switch to the **YSlow** tab.

3. Click on the **Run Test** button to fire off the main test. This runs through a number of tests before producing a list of its findings:

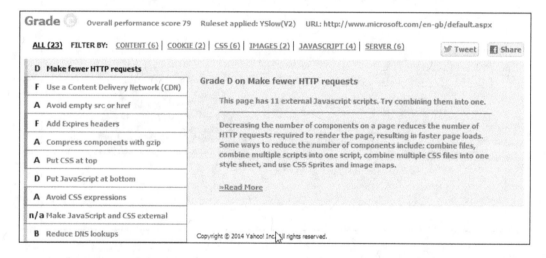

4. We're interested in the tests that relate to images, so click on **IMAGES (2)** to filter the results.

Now that we've seen the results of the scan, let's analyze some of the results.

Analyzing results

Take, for example, the following entry:

```
http://c.s-microsoft.com/en-gb/CMSImages/SpringPromo_
LastFrameBG_1600x540_EN_US.jpg?version=250bf4d8-ad95-96e7-3b61-
394b95449a92
```

This happens to be the first on the list; it is the main one displayed immediately below the menu bar:

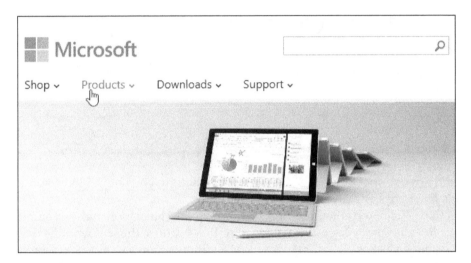

This is a perfect example of how it has failed the test for YSlow. The original image has been scaled, which puts extra demand on the server when rendering it on screen down to 1366 x 461 px:

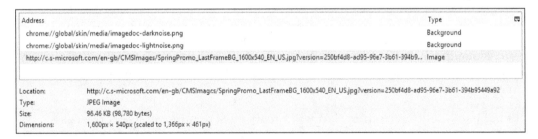

This seems perfectly reasonable. Scaling down an image will put extra demand on the server.

Digging further into the code

Hold on! Something doesn't add up here. If we dig further by using Firebug to check the CSS styles, we can see the styles applied in the following screenshot. In this instance, it's an example of `.hero .image .media` and `.hero .img video`:

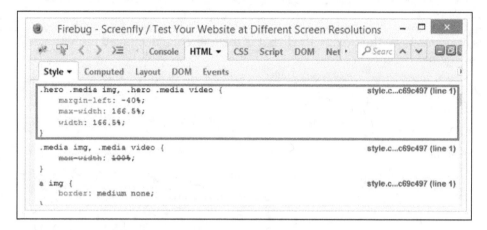

Now, did anyone spot anything? The keen-eyed among you should have spotted that this image has already appeared earlier in the *Testing responsive sites with online tools* section. There, we noted that the site appeared to be responsive—dynamic percentage values have been used, instead of fixed values; this we would expect to see on responsive sites. So, what gives? Why, with percentage values, are we still seeing issues being reported by YSlow?

Revealing all

Well, to find out why, we need to dig further into the CSS file being used on `http://www.microsoft.com`. In the screenshot from Firebug, did you notice the `166.5%` value against `max-width`? And that this is overriding a `max-width` value of `100%` immediately below? Therein lies our first clue—back in *Chapter 1, Working with Responsive Images*, I mentioned that the basic and easiest way to create responsive images is to set a `max-width` value of `100%`.

It's not without its own quirks, but will satisfy most requirements—at least as a starting point to implementing responsive behavior. So why do we have a value that is over 50 percent higher?

The true answer to this lies in the CSS file. A search of it using a text editor, such as Sublime Text, would appear to show that media queries have been used. This we would expect to see. But where the design has fallen over is in how the images have been set to display on the page.

The image we've selected is only set once. None of the media queries have been set to replace the image with a smaller one if the viewport or browser window size is reduced—therein lies the problem!

Fixing the problem

While we clearly do not have access to alter the code, we can at least work out the steps required to fix the problem:

1. In Firefox, right-click on the image and click on **View Image Info** to view the properties.

   In this exercise, I will assume you are using GIMP for Windows. If you are using a different package, please adjust the steps accordingly.

   This screenshot shows the page resized to the smallest width possible in Firefox:

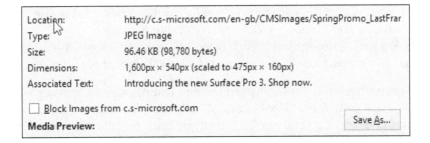

2. Click on **Save As...** to save a copy locally—the name is not critical; open it in an image editing application, such as PhotoShop or GIMP.

3. When opened, it will show at full size, which is **1600px x 540px**; navigate to **Image | Scale Image...** and set the new size to **475px x 160px**. Click on **Scale** to resize the image.

4. Next, go to **File | Overwrite...** to update the image. On **Export Image as JPEG**, push the Quality scale to **100%** if it is not already set at this value.

5. Click on **Export** to complete the process—the image will now be saved to the new dimensions.

At this point, we have an updated image, which would normally be uploaded to the website. A quick check shows that it has been reduced from a hefty 96 KB down to a more reasonable 38 KB. This makes it quicker to download in our style sheet.

Of course, to really finish it off though, we would need to include a media query in our style sheet that makes use of the smaller image when the viewport has been suitably resized, such as the following lines of code:

```
@media screen and (max-width: 475px) {
....
   .hero.media img {
     background: url(<path and name of new file>) no repeat;
   ...
   }
}
```

Not only does this mean that we're reducing the amount of content to download, but we're also removing some of the demand on the server and helping to make the response time of the site snappier – a win-win for all concerned! It takes a little research and planning to achieve this. But once implemented, it will dramatically reduce the overall effort required to make our media content responsive.

Summary

Website testing is one of the key steps to creating online sites. This is our chance to ensure that images and videos resize properly and that content appears correctly in our responsive sites. Throughout this chapter, we've taken a look at how we should test responsive content. Let's take a moment to consider what we have learned.

We kicked off with a look at the simplest form of testing, using the usual desktop browsers. We saw how this will take care of the basics, but that we can complement it using online services that can emulate multiple browsers at the same time.

Next up came a look at some of the pitfalls of responsive site testing; we learned how the most effective way to test is doing it manually. There are too many inconsistencies that make any form of automation difficult.

Moving swiftly on, we then turned our attention to using online tools to test responsive content – we saw how they work in a similar fashion to the responsive features in desktop browsers, but can offer a wider range of facilities. We then rounded out the chapter with a look at testing of responsive sites. We saw how with YSlow, we can soon identify slow responding elements; we then worked through a theoretical example to see what would happen and how we could fix it if we were the owner of the site.

Phew! It may have only been a short chapter, but we covered a lot! In the next one, we'll be taking a look at applying some of the principles that we've covered throughout the book to CMS systems such as WordPress.

5
Using Frameworks

Throughout this book, we've covered a number of tips and tricks we can use to add media to our responsive sites, which includes both images and video. These are good, but how do they work in real life?

Let's answer that now. We can't fail to note the rapid rise of three popular frameworks, namely Less CSS, WordPress, and of course Twitter's Bootstrap. These are used in thousands of sites worldwide—certainly not something to be sniffed at! In this chapter, we're going to work through some simple examples that use these tools to show how we can apply some of the techniques that we've covered so far in the book.

Over the next few pages, we will cover the following topics:

- Adding responsive media to a CMS
- Implementing responsive media in frameworks such as Twitter Bootstrap
- Using the Less CSS preprocessor to create CSS media queries

Ready? Let's make a start!

Introducing our three examples

Throughout this book, we've covered a number of simple, practical techniques to make media responsive within our sites—these are good, but nothing beats seeing these principles used in a real-world context, right?

Absolutely! To prove this, we're going to look at three examples throughout this chapter, using technologies that you are likely to be familiar with: WordPress, Bootstrap, and Less CSS. Each demo will assume a certain level of prior knowledge, so it may be worth reading up a little first. In all three cases, we should see that with little effort, we can easily add responsive media to each one of these technologies. Let's kick off with a look at working with WordPress.

Adding responsive media to a CMS

We will begin the first of our three examples with a look at using the ever popular WordPress system. Created back in 2003, WordPress has been used to host sites by small independent traders all the way up to Fortune 500 companies—this includes some of the biggest names in business such as eBay, UPS, and Ford. WordPress comes in two flavors; the one we're interested in is the self-install version available at `http://www.wordpress.org`.

This example assumes you have a local installation of WordPress installed and working; if not, then head over to `http://codex.wordpress.org/Installing_WordPress` and follow the tutorial to get started. We will also need a DOM inspector such as Firebug installed if you don't already have it. It can be downloaded from `http://www.getfirebug.com` if you need to install it.

> If you only have access to WordPress.com (the other flavor of WordPress), then some of the tips in this section may not work, due to limitations in that version of WordPress.

Okay, assuming we have WordPress set up and running, let's make a start on making uploaded media responsive.

Adding responsive media manually

If we cast our minds back to *Chapter 1*, *Working with Responsive Images*, we discovered that in most cases, it was sufficient to simply set `max-width: 100%` against any image that we wanted to be responsive.

It's at this point that you're probably thinking we have to do something complex when working in WordPress, right? Wrong! As long as you use the Twenty Fourteen core theme, the work has already been done for you.

> For this exercise, and the following sections, I will assume you have installed and/or activated WordPress' Twenty Fourteen theme.

Don't believe me? It's easy to verify: try uploading an image to a post or page in WordPress. Resize the browser — you should see the image shrink or grow in size as the browser window changes size. If we take a peek at WordPress under the covers, using a DOM Inspector such as Firebug, we can easily see how the code is no different to that back in *Chapter 1, Working with Responsive Images.*

```
.comment-content img, .entry-content img,    style.css?ver=4.0 (line 571)
.entry-summary img, #site-header img,
.widget img, .wp-caption {
    max-width: 100%;
}
```

If we take a look at the code elsewhere using Firebug, we can also see the `height: auto` set against a number of the `img` tags; this is frequently done for responsive images to ensure they maintain the correct proportions.

The responsive style seems to work well in the Twenty Fourteen theme; if you are using an older theme, we can easily apply the same style rule to images stored in WordPress when using that theme.

Fixing a responsive issue

So far, so good. Now, we have the Twenty Fourteen theme in place, we've uploaded images of various sizes, and we try resizing the browser window ... only to find that the images don't seem to grow in size above a certain point. At least not well — what gives?

Well, it's a classic trap: we've talked about using percentage values to dynamically resize images, only to find that we've shot ourselves in the foot (proverbially speaking, of course!). The reason? Let's dive in and find out using the following steps:

1. Browse to your WordPress installation and activate Firebug using *F12.*

2. Switch to the **HTML** tab and select your preferred image.

3. In Firebug, look for the `<header class="entry-header">` line, then look for the following line in the rendered styles on the right-hand side of the window:

   ```
   .site-content .entry-header, .site-content .entry-content,
     .site-content .entry-summary, .site-content .entry-meta,
     .page-content {
       margin: 0 auto; max-width: 474px;
   }
   ```

4. The keen-eyed amongst you should hopefully spot the issue straightaway — we're using percentages to make the sizes dynamic for each image, yet we're constraining its parent container! To fix this, change the highlighted line as indicated:

```
.site-content .entry-header, .site-content .entry-content,
  .site-content .entry-summary, .site-content .entry-meta,
  .page-content {
    margin: 0 auto; max-width: 100%;
}
```

5. To balance the content, we need to make the same change to the comments area. So go ahead and change max-width to 100% as follows:

```
.comments-area { margin: 48px auto; max-width: 100%;
  padding: 0 10px; }
```

6. If we try resizing the browser window now, we should see the image size adjust automatically.

At this stage, the change is not permanent. To fix this, we would log in to WordPress' admin area, go to **Appearance | Editor** and add the adjusted styles at the foot of the **Stylesheet (style.css)** file.

Let's move on. Did anyone notice two rather critical issues with the approach used here? Hopefully, you must have spotted that if a large image is used and then resized to a smaller size, we're still working with large files. The alteration we're making has a big impact on the theme, even though it is only a small change. Even though it proves that we can make images truly responsive, it is the kind of change that we would not necessarily want to make without careful consideration and plenty of testing.

We can improve on this. However, making changes directly to the CSS style sheet is not ideal; they could be lost when upgrading to a newer version of the theme. We can improve on this by either using a custom CSS plugin to manage these changes or (better) using a plugin that tells WordPress to swap an existing image for a small one automatically if we resize the window to a smaller size.

Using plugins to add responsive images

A drawback though, of using a theme such as Twenty Fourteen, is the resizing of images. While we can grow or shrink an image when resizing the browser window, we are still technically altering the size of what could potentially be an unnecessarily large image!

This is considered bad practice (and also bad manners!) — browsing on a desktop with a fast Internet connection as it might not have too much of an impact; the same cannot be said for mobile devices, where we have less choice.

To overcome this, we need to take a different approach — get WordPress to automatically swap in smaller images when we reach a particular size or breakpoint. Instead of doing this manually using code, we can take advantage of one of the many plugins available that offer responsive capabilities in some format.

I feel a demo coming on. Now's a good time to take a look at one such plugin in action:

1. Let's start by downloading our plugin. For this exercise, we'll use the `PictureFill.WP` plugin by Kyle Ricks, which is available at `https://wordpress.org/plugins/picturefillwp/`. We're going to use the version that uses `Picturefill.js` version 2. This is available to download from `https://github.com/kylereicks/picturefill.js.wp/tree/master`. Click on **Download ZIP** to get the latest version.

2. Log in to the admin area of your WordPress installation and click on **Settings** and then **Media**. Make sure your image settings for **Thumbnail**, **Medium**, and **Large** sizes are set to values that work with useful breakpoints in your design.

3. We then need to install the plugin. In the admin area, go to **Plugins | Add New** to install the plugin and activate it in the normal manner.

   At this point, we will have installed responsive capabilities in WordPress — everything is managed automatically by the plugin; there is no need to change any settings (except maybe the image sizes we talked about in step 2).

4. Switch back to your WordPress frontend and try resizing the screen to a smaller size.

5. Press *F12* to activate Firebug and switch to the **HTML** tab.

6. Press *Ctrl* + *Shift* + *C* (or *Cmd* + *Shift* + *C* for Mac users) to toggle the element inspector; move your mouse over your resized image.

7. If we've set the right image sizes in WordPress' admin area and the window is resized correctly, we can expect to see something like the following screenshot:

```
<p>
  <a href="http://localhost/wordpress/wp-content/uploads/2014/09/orchids-large.png">
    <img class="alignnone wp-image-28" width="674" height="449" srcset="http://localhost
    /wordpress/wp-content/uploads/2014/09/orchids-large-150x150.png 150w,
    http://localhost/wordpress/wp-content/uploads/2014/09/orchids-large-300x200.png
    300w, http://localhost/wordpress/wp-content/uploads/2014/09/orchids-large-
    1024x682.png 1024w, http://localhost/wordpress/wp-content/uploads/2014/09/orchids-
    large.png 1944w" sizes="(max-width: 674px) 100vw, 674px" alt="orchids-
    large" src="http://localhost/wordpress/wp-content/uploads/2014/09/orchids-large-
    300x200.png">
  </a>
</p>
```

8. To confirm we are indeed using a smaller image, right-click on the image and select **View Image Info**; it will display something akin to the following screenshot:

Location:	http://localhost/wordpress/wp-content/uploads/2014/09/orchids-large-300x200.png
Type:	PNG Image
Size:	114.06 KB (116,800 bytes)
Dimensions:	300px × 200px (scaled to 265px × 177px)
Associated Text:	orchids-large

We should now have a fully functioning plugin within our WordPress installation. A good tip is to test this thoroughly, if only to ensure we've set the right sizes for our breakpoints in WordPress!

What happens if WordPress doesn't refresh my thumbnail images properly?

This can happen. If you find this happening, get hold of and install the Regenerate Thumbnails plugin to resolve this issue; it's available at https://wordpress.org/plugins/regenerate-thumbnails/.

Adding responsive videos using plugins

Now that we can add responsive images to WordPress, let's turn our attention to videos. The process of adding them is a little more complex; we need to use code to achieve the best effect. Let's examine our options.

If you are hosting your own videos, the simplest way is to add some additional CSS style rules. Although this removes any reliance on JavaScript or jQuery using this method, the result isn't perfect and will need additional styles to handle the repositioning of the play button overlay.

 Although we are working locally, we should remember the note from earlier in the chapter; changes to the CSS style sheet may be lost when upgrading. A custom CSS plugin should be used, if possible, to retain any changes.

To use a CSS-only solution, it only requires a couple of steps:

1. Browse to your WordPress theme folder and open a copy of `styles.css` in your text editor of choice.

2. Add the following lines at the end of the file and save it:

```
video { width: 100%; height: 100%; max-width: 100%; }
.wp-video { width: 100% !important; }
.wp-video-shortcode {width: 100% !important; }
```

3. Close the file. You now have the basics in place for responsive videos.

At this stage, you're probably thinking, "great, my videos are now responsive. I can handle the repositioning of the play button overlay myself, no problem"; sounds about right?

Thought so and therein lies the main drawback of this method! Repositioning the overlay shouldn't be too difficult. The real problem is in the high costs of hardware and bandwidth that is needed to host videos of any reasonable quality and that even if we were to spend time repositioning the overlay, the high costs would outweigh any benefit of using a CSS-only solution.

A far better option is to let a service such as YouTube do all the hard work for you and to simply embed your chosen video directly from YouTube into your pages. The main benefit of this is that YouTube's servers do all the hard work for you. You can take advantage of an increased audience and YouTube will automatically optimize the video for the best resolution possible for the Internet connections being used by your visitors.

 Although aimed at beginners, wpbeginner.com has a useful article located at `http://www.wpbeginner.com/beginners-guide/why-you-should-never-upload-a-video-to-wordpress/`, on the pros and cons of why self-hosting videos isn't recommended and that using an external service is preferable.

Using plugins to embed videos

Embedding videos from an external service into WordPress is ironically far simpler than using the CSS method. There are dozens of plugins available to achieve this, but one of the simplest to use (and my personal favorite) is FluidVids, by Todd Motto, available at `http://github.com/toddmotto/fluidvids/`.

To get it working in WordPress, we need to follow these steps using a video from YouTube as the basis for our example:

1. Browse to your WordPress' theme folder and open a copy of `functions.php` in your usual text editor.

2. At the bottom, add the following lines:

```
add_action ( 'wp_enqueue_scripts', 'add_fluidvid' );

function add_fluidvid() {
  wp_enqueue_script ( 'fluidvids',
    get_stylesheet_directory_uri() .
    '/lib/js/fluidvids.js', array(), false, true );
}
```

3. Save the file, then log in to the admin area of your WordPress installation.

4. Navigate to **Posts** | **Add New** to add a post and switch to the **Text** tab of your Post Editor, then add `http://www.youtube.com/watch?v=Vpg9yizPP_g&hd=1` to the editor on the page.

5. Click on **Update** to save your post, then click on **View post** to see the video in action.

There is no need to further configure WordPress—any video added from services such as YouTube or Vimeo will be automatically set as responsive by the FluidVids plugin. At this point, try resizing the browser window. If all is well, we should see the video shrink or grow in size, depending on how the browser window has been resized:

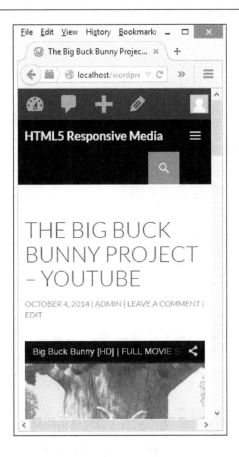

To prove that the code is working, we can take a peek at the compiled results within Firebug. We will see something akin to the following screenshot:

```
<script src="http://localhost/wordpress/wp-content/themes/twentyfourteen
   /js/functions.js?ver=20140319" type="text/javascript">
<script src="http://localhost/wordpress/wp-content/themes/twentyfourteen
   /js/fluidvids.js?ver=4.0" type="text/javascript">
<script type="text/javascript">
<div id="wpadminbar" class="" role="navigation">
```

For those of us who are not feeling quite so brave (!), there is fortunately a WordPress plugin available that will achieve the same results, without configuration. It's available at `https://wordpress.org/plugins/fluidvids/` and can be downloaded and installed using the normal process for WordPress plugins.

Let's change track and move onto our next demo. I feel a need to get stuck in some coding, so let's take a look at how we can implement responsive images in frameworks such as Bootstrap.

Implementing responsive media in Bootstrap

A question — as developers, hands up if you have not heard of Bootstrap? Good — not too many hands going down

Why have I asked this question, I hear you say? Easy — it's to illustrate that in popular frameworks (such as Bootstrap), it is easy to add basic responsive capabilities to media, such as images or video. The exact process may differ from framework to framework, but the result is likely to be very similar. To see what I mean, let's take a look at using Bootstrap for our second demo, where we'll see just how easy it is to add images and video to our Bootstrap-enabled site.

 If you would like to explore using some of the free Bootstrap templates that are available, then `http://www.startbootstrap.com/` is well worth a visit!

Using Bootstrap's CSS classes

Making images and videos responsive in Bootstrap uses a slightly different approach to what we've examined so far; this is only because we don't have to define each style property explicitly, but instead simply add the appropriate class to the media HTML for it to render responsively.

For the purposes of this demo, we'll use an edited version of the Blog Page example, available at `http://www.getbootstrap.com/getting-started/#examples`; a copy of the edited version is available on the code download that accompanies this book. Before we begin, go ahead and download a copy of the Bootstrap Example folder that is in the code download. Inside, you'll find the CSS, image and JavaScript files needed, along with our HTML markup file.

Now that we have our files, the following is a screenshot of what we're going to achieve over the course of our demo:

Let's make a start on our example using the following steps:

1. Open up `bootstrap.html` and look for the following lines (around lines 34 to 35):

    ```
    <p class="blog-post-meta">January 1, 2014 by <a
        href="#">Mark</a></p>
        <p>This blog post shows a few different types of
            content that's supported and styled with Bootstrap.
            Basic typography, images, and code are all
            supported.</p>
    ```

2. Immediately below, add the following code—this contains markup for our embedded video, using Bootstrap's responsive CSS styling:

    ```
    <div class="bs-example">
      <div class="embed-responsive embed-responsive-16by9">
        <iframe allowfullscreen=""
            src="http://www.youtube.com/embed/zpOULjyy-n8?rel=0"
            class="embed-responsive-item"></iframe>
      </div>
    </div>
    ```

3. With the video now styled, let's go ahead and add in an image — this will go in the **About** section on the right. Look for these lines, on or around lines 74 and 75:

    ```
    <h4>About</h4>
     <p>Etiam porta <em>sem malesuada magna</em> mollis
     euismod. Cras mattis consectetur purus sit amet
     fermentum. Aenean lacinia bibendum nulla sed
     consectetur.</p>
    ```

4. Immediately below, add in the following markup for our image:

    ```
    <a href="#" class="thumbnail">
      <img src="http://placehold.it/350x150" class="img-
        responsive">
    </a>
    ```

5. Save the file and preview the results in a browser. If all is well, we can see our video and image appear, as shown at the start of our demo.

At this point, try resizing the browser — you should see the video and placeholder image shrink or grow as the window is resized. However, the great thing about Bootstrap is that the right styles have already been set for each class. All we need to do is apply the correct class to the appropriate media file — `.embed-responsive embed-responsive-16by9` for videos or `.img-responsive for images` — for that image or video to behave responsively within our site.

 In this example, we used Bootstrap's `.img-responsive` class in the code; if we have a lot of images, we could consider using `img { max-width: 100%; height: auto; }` instead.

So far, we've worked with two popular examples of frameworks in the form of WordPress and Bootstrap. This is great, but it can mean getting stuck into a lot of CSS styling, particularly if we're working with media queries, as we saw earlier in the book! Can we do anything about this? Absolutely! It's time for a brief look at CSS preprocessing and how this can help with adding responsive media to our pages.

Using Less CSS to create responsive content

Working with frameworks often means getting stuck into a lot of CSS styling; this can become awkward to manage if we're not careful! To help with this, and for our third scenario, we're going back to basics to work on an alternative way of rendering CSS using the Less CSS preprocessing language.

Why? Well, as a superset (or extension) of CSS, Less allows us to write our styles more efficiently; it then compiles them into valid CSS. The aim of this example is to show that if you're already using Less, then we can still apply the same principles that we've covered throughout this book, to make our content responsive.

 It should be noted that this exercise does assume a certain level of prior experience using Less; if this is the first time, you may like to peruse my book, *Learning Less*, by Packt Publishing.

To see what I mean—let's rework the responsive demo from *Chapter 3, Mixing Content*, where we mixed both video and images to use Less in place of normal CSS. There will be a few steps involved in making the changes, so the following screenshot gives a heads-up on what it will look like, once we've finished:

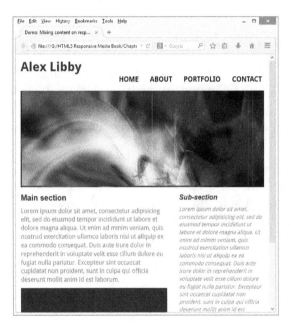

Hold on! the keen-eyed amongst you might notice that there is nothing different between this version and the one from *Chapter 3, Mixing Content*.

You would be right. If we play our cards right, there should indeed be no change in appearance; working with Less is all about writing CSS more efficiently. Let's see what is involved:

1. We'll start by extracting copies of the Less CSS example from the code download that accompanies this book—inside it, we'll find our HTML markup, reset style sheet, images, and video needed for our demo. Save the folder locally to your PC.

2. Next, add the following styles in a new file, saving it as `responsive.less` in the `css` subfolder — we'll start with some of the styling for the base elements, such as the video and banner:

```
#wrapper {width: 96%; max-width: 45rem; margin: auto;
  padding: 2%}
#main { width: 60%; margin-right: 5%; float: left }
#video-wrapper video { max-width:  100%; }
#banner { background-image: url('../img/abstract-banner-
  large.jpg'); height: 15.31rem; width: 45.5rem; max-width:
  100%;
float: left; margin-bottom: 15px; }
#skipTo { display: none; li { background: #197a8a }; }

p { font-family: "Droid Sans",sans-serif; }
aside { width: 35%; float: right; }
footer { border-top: 1px solid #ccc; clear: both; height:
  30px; padding-top: 5px; }
```

3. We need to add some basic formatting styles for images and links, so go ahead and add the following, immediately below the `#skipTo` rule:

```
a { text-decoration: none; text-transform: uppercase }
a, img { border: medium none; color: #000; font-weight: bold;
outline: medium none; }
```

4. Next up comes the navigation for our page. These styles control the main navigation and the **Skip To...** link that appears when viewed on smaller devices. Go ahead and add these style rules immediately below the rules for a and img:

```
header {
  font-family: 'Droid Sans', sans-serif;
  h1 { height: 70px; float: left; display: block; font-
    weight: 700; font-size: 2rem; }
  nav {
    float: right; margin-top: 40px; height: 22px; border-
      radius: 4px;
    li { display: inline; margin-left: 15px; }
    ul { font-weight: 400; font-size: 1.1rem; }
    a {
      padding: 5px 5px 5px 5px;
      &:hover { background-color: #27a7bd; color: #fff; border-
radius: 4px; }
    }
  }
}
```

5. We need to add the media query that controls the display for smaller devices, so go ahead and add the following to a new file and save it as media.less in the css subfolder. We'll start with setting the screen size for our media query:

```
@smallscreen: ~"screen and (max-width: 30rem)";

@media @smallscreen {
  p { font-family: "Droid Sans", sans-serif; }

  #main, aside { margin: 0 0 10px; width: 100%; }
  #banner { margin-top: 150px; height: 4.85rem; max-
    width: 100%; background-image: url('../img/abstract-
    banner-medium.jpg'); width: 45.5rem; }
```

6. Next up comes the media query rule that will handle the **Skip To...** link at the top of our resized window:

```
#skipTo {
  display: block; height: 18px;
  a {
    display: block; text-align: center; color: #fff;
      font-size: 0.8rem;
    &:hover { background-color: #27a7bd; border-radius:
      0; height: 20px }
  }
}
```

7. We can't forget the main navigation, so go ahead and add the following line of code immediately below the block for #skipTo:

```
header {
  h1 { margin-top: 20px }
  nav {
    float: left; clear: left; margin: 0 0 10px; width:
      100%;
    li { margin: 0; background: #efefef; display:
      block; margin-bottom: 3px; height: 40px; }
    a {
      display: block; padding: 10px; text-align:
        center; color: #000;
      &:hover {background-color: #27a7bd; border-
        radius: 0; padding: 10px; height: 20px; }
    }
  }
}
```

At this point, we should then compile the Less style sheet before previewing the results of our work. If we launch `responsive.html` in a browser, we'll see our mocked up portfolio page appear as we saw at the beginning of the exercise. If we resize the screen to its minimum width, its responsive design kicks in to reorder and resize elements on screen, as we would expect to see.

Okay, so we now have a responsive page that uses Less CSS for styling; it still seems like a lot of code, right?

Working through the code in detail

Although this seems like a lot of code for a simple page, the principles we've used are in fact very simple and are the ones we already used earlier in the book. Not convinced? Well, let's look at it in more detail—the focus of this book is on responsive images and video, so we'll start with video.

Open the `responsive.css` style sheet and look for the `#video-wrapper` video class:

```
#video-wrapper video { max-width:  100%; }
```

Notice how it's set to a `max-width` value of `100%`? We used `max-width` to style the original video back in *Chapter 2, Adding Responsive Video Content*. It's no different here. Granted, we don't want to resize a large video to a really small size—we would use a media query to replace it with a smaller version. But, for most purposes, `max-width` should be sufficient.

Now, for the image, this is a little more complicated, but it still uses the same principles we applied back in *Chapter 1, Working with Responsive Images*. Let's start with the code from `responsive.less`:

```
#banner { background-image: url('../img/abstract-banner-
   large.jpg'); height: 15.31rem; width: 45.5rem; max-width: 100%;
float: left; margin-bottom: 15px; }
```

Here, we used the `max-width` value again, exactly as we did back in *Chapter 1, Working with Responsive Images*. In both instances, we can style the element directly, unlike videos where we have to add a container in order to style it. The theme continues in the media query setup in `media.less`:

```
@smallscreen: ~"screen and (max-width: 30rem)";
@media @smallscreen {
  ...
  #banner { margin-top: 150px; background-image:
    url('../img/abstract-banner-medium.jpg'); height: 4.85rem;
    width: 45.5rem; max-width: 100%; }
  ...
}
```

In this instance, we're styling the element to cover the width of the viewport, in exactly the same way as we did back in *Chapter 3*, *Mixing Content*.

A small point of note; you might ask why we are using the `rem` values instead of the percentage values when styling our image? This is a good question—the key to it is that when using pixel values, these do not scale well in responsive designs. However, the `rem` values do scale beautifully; we could use percentage values if we're so inclined, although they are best suited to instances where we need to fill a container that only covers part of the screen (as we did with the video for this demo).

An interesting article extolling the virtues of why we should use rem units is available at `http://techtime.getharvest.com/blog/in-defense-of-rem-units` - it's worth a read. Of particular note is a known bug with using rem values in Mobile Safari, which should be considered when developing for mobile platforms; with all of the iPhones available, its usage could be said to be higher than Firefox! For more details, head over to `http://wtfhtmlcss.com/#rems-mobile-safari`.

Transferring to production use

Throughout this exercise, we used Less to compile our styles on the fly each time. This is okay for development purposes, but is not recommended for production use. Once we've worked out the requisite styles needed for our site, we should always look to precompile them into valid CSS before uploading the results into our site.

There are a number of options available for this purpose; two of my personal favorites are Crunch! available at `http://www.crunchapp.net` and the Less2CSS plugin for Sublime Text available at `https://github.com/timdouglas/sublime-less2css`.

You can learn more about precompiling Less code from my new book, *Learning Less.js*, by Packt Publishing.

Summary

Wow! We've certainly covered a lot; it shows that adding basic responsive capabilities to media need not be difficult. Let's take a moment to recap on what you learned.

We kicked off this chapter with an introduction to three real-word scenarios that we would then cover. Our first scenario looked at using WordPress. We covered how although we can add simple CSS styling to make images and videos responsive, the preferred method is to use one of the several plugins available to achieve the same result.

Our next scenario visited the all too familiar framework known as Twitter Bootstrap. In comparison, we saw that this is a much easier framework to work with, in that styles have been predefined and that all we needed to do was add the right class to the right selector.

Our third and final scenario went completely the opposite way, with a look at using the Less CSS preprocessor to handle the styles that we would otherwise have manually created. We saw how easy it was to rework the styles we originally created earlier in the chapter to produce a more concise and efficient version that compiled into valid CSS with no apparent change in design.

Well, we've now reached the end of the book; all good things must come to an end at some point! Nonetheless, I hope you've enjoyed reading the book as much as I have writing it. Hopefully, I've shown that adding responsive media to your sites need not be as complicated as it might first look and that it gives you a good grounding to develop something more complex using responsive media.

Index

responsive media, implementing
in Bootstrap 102

F

fallback support
  catering to 46-48
Firebug
  URL 87, 94
Firefogg applet
  URL 41
Firefox
  using 79
FitVids.js
  URL 48
fluid images 8-10
FluidVids
  URL 49, 100
Font Awesome icons
  URL 31
Fontello service 71
format support
  URL 64
FrescoJS
  URL 62

G

GIMP
  URL 27
Google Chrome
  using 78
Google Maps
  used, for creating responsive maps 34, 35
Grunt
  URL 13
Grunt plugin
  URL 52

H

Handbrake
  URL 41
HD
  catering to 12, 13
high-resolution (hi-res) 12

I

image content
  and video content, mixing on
    same page 60-62
image formats 10
image icons
  using, for scalability 30-32
Internet Explorer
  using 80, 81

J

JavaScript
  used, for setting viewport 18, 19
jQuery
  URL 22
JS
  used, for determining page
    breakpoints 22-24
JS libraries
  using, to provide support 48, 49

L

lazy loading
  about 68
  adding, to pages 67-69
Less2CSS plugin
  URL 109
Less CSS
  code, working through 108, 109
  production use, transferring to 109
  used, for creating responsive
    content 104-108
low-resolution (low-res) devices 12

M

Marriot
  URL 82
media queries 20-22
mixing content
  pitfalls 63-65
mobile devices
  responsive images, creating
    automatically 72-74

responsive images, mixing 70-72
shrinking process, automating 74, 75
videos, mixing 70-72
Mobile Safari
URL 109
Modernizr
URL 11

N

Network API
URL 11
Node
URL 52
Node JS
installing 72

O

online tools
used, for testing responsive sites 83-87
OpenDeviceLab.com 86
Opera
using 78, 79

P

page breakpoints
determining, pure JS used 22-24
pages
lazy loading support, adding 67-69
pixels per inch (PPI) 12
Placehold.it service
URL 24
platforms
catering to 11
plugins
used, for adding responsive images 96-98
used, for adding responsive videos 98, 99
used, for embedding videos 100-102
preloaders
used, for reducing delays 65-67
PreloadJS
URL 65
PT Sans font
URL 16

R

Regenerate Thumbnails plugin
URL 98
rem units
URL 109
responsImg
URL 13
Responsinator
URL 86
responsive carousel
building 32, 33
responsive content
creating, Less CSS used 104-108
Responsive Design Checker
URL 86
responsive images
adding, plugins used 96-98
creating, automatically 72-74
displaying, sprites used 13-15
URL 11, 27
responsive maps
creating, Google Maps used 34, 35
responsive media
adding, manually 94, 95
adding, to CMS 94
implementing, in Bootstrap 102
responsive issue, fixing 95, 96
responsive sites
testing, online tools used 83-87
ResponsiveSlides library
URL 32
responsive sprite image creator
URL 14
responsive testing
pitfalls 81, 83
responsive tool
URL 11
responsive video content
<video> formats, support determining 39
about 38
different platforms, catering to 49-51
fallback support, catering to 46-48
full-size videos, displaying 54-57
HTML5 video content, embedding 41-43
JS libraries, used for support 48, 49
right format, selecting 39-41

URL 49
vendor prefixes, allowing for 52-54
viewport available for use,
    determining 44-46
responsive videos
adding, plugins used 98, 99
retina images
catering to 12, 13
RetinaJS library
URL 13

S

scalability
image icons, used 30-32
SVG image format, working with 28-30
ScreenFly emulator
URL 84
SimpleVid
URL 49
speed determination
code 90, 91
issues, fixing 91, 92
results, analyzing 89
tools used 87, 88
sprites
used, for displaying responsive
    images 13-15
SVG image format
working with, for scalability 28-30
SVG images
URL 30

T

testing
about 77, 78
Firefox used 79
Google Chrome used 78, 79
Internet Explorer used 80, 81
Opera used 78, 79
third-party embedded videos
URL 62
tools
used, for determining speed 87, 88
Tribilis
URL 63

U

Unicode Private Use Areas
about 32
URL 32

V

vendor prefixes
about 10
allowing for 52-54
videos
content and image content, mixing on
    same page 62
embedding, plugins used 100-102
viewport
available for use, determining 44-46
for use, determining 15
getting, JavaScript used 18, 19
setting, CSS used 16, 17
URL 15
Viewport Resizer
URL 86

W

WordPress
URL 94
WOW Slider
URL 33
wpbeginner.com
article, URL 99

X

XMedia Recode
URL 40
XOO.me
URL 28

About Packt Publishing

Packt, pronounced 'packed', published its first book, *Mastering phpMyAdmin for Effective MySQL Management*, in April 2004, and subsequently continued to specialize in publishing highly focused books on specific technologies and solutions.

Our books and publications share the experiences of your fellow IT professionals in adapting and customizing today's systems, applications, and frameworks. Our solution-based books give you the knowledge and power to customize the software and technologies you're using to get the job done. Packt books are more specific and less general than the IT books you have seen in the past. Our unique business model allows us to bring you more focused information, giving you more of what you need to know, and less of what you don't.

Packt is a modern yet unique publishing company that focuses on producing quality, cutting-edge books for communities of developers, administrators, and newbies alike. For more information, please visit our website at www.packtpub.com.

Writing for Packt

We welcome all inquiries from people who are interested in authoring. Book proposals should be sent to author@packtpub.com. If your book idea is still at an early stage and you would like to discuss it first before writing a formal book proposal, then please contact us; one of our commissioning editors will get in touch with you.

We're not just looking for published authors; if you have strong technical skills but no writing experience, our experienced editors can help you develop a writing career, or simply get some additional reward for your expertise.

HTML5 and CSS3 Responsive Web Design Cookbook

ISBN: 978-1-84969-544-2   Paperback: 204 pages

Learn the secrets of developing responsive websites capable of interfacing with today's mobile Internet devices

1. Learn the fundamental elements of writing responsive website code for all stages of the development life cycle.

2. Create the ultimate code writer's resource using logical workflow layers.

3. Full of usable code for immediate use in your website projects.

4. Written in an easy-to-understand language giving knowledge without preaching.

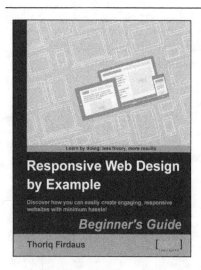

Responsive Web Design by Example Beginner's Guide

ISBN: 978-1-84969-542-8   Paperback: 338 pages

Discover how you can easily create engaging, responsive websites with minimum hassle!

1. Rapidly develop and prototype responsive websites by utilizing powerful open source frameworks.

2. Focus less on the theory and more on results, with clear step-by-step instructions, previews, and examples to help you along the way.

3. Learn how you can utilize three of the most powerful responsive frameworks available today: Bootstrap, Skeleton, and Zurb Foundation.

Please check **www.PacktPub.com** for information on our titles

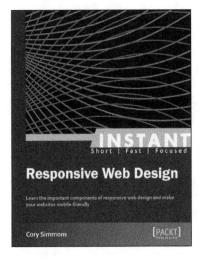

Instant Responsive Web Design

ISBN: 978-1-84969-925-9   Paperback: 70 pages

Learn the important components of responsive web design and make your websites mobile-friendly

1. Learn something new in an Instant! A short, fast, focused guide delivering immediate results.

2. Learn how to make your websites beautiful on any device.

3. Understand the differences between various responsive philosophies.

4. Expand your skill set with the quickly growing mobile-first approach.

Mastering HTML5 Forms

ISBN: 978-1-78216-466-1   Paperback: 148 pages

Create dynamic and responsive web forms with this in-depth, hands-on guide

1. Enhance the look and feel of your form.

2. Optimize your user experience for any device.

3. Utilize HTML5's brand new form elements.

Please check **www.PacktPub.com** for information on our titles

www.ingramcontent.com/pod-product-compliance
Lightning Source LLC
LaVergne TN
LVHW080100070326
832902LV00014B/2329